The Year of the Tiger
Adelaide McLeod, Raconteuse

True Confessions of a Real Estate Broker

Copyright 2015 by Adelaide McLeod

ISBN 978-0-990-3680-8-7

The Year of the Tiger

The Way it Was

"Vegetables! Vegetables!" Wong called in his twangy sing-song voice as he guided his Model-T truck down our orange-sand alley. Bobby Oliver and I ran after him and jumped on the back bumper and held on for dear life as it jerked and bumped its way along. Wong was very tall for a Chinese man; he had a long face and twinkling eyes.

"What do you suppose Wong brought today?" I asked Bobby.

"I don't know, but I don't like vegetables. Is that all he has?" Bobby asked.

"Yes, but you'd like vegetables if your mom fixed them the way my mom does with lots of butter and spices."

Wong's produce was hidden behind a roll-up canvas curtain grown tattered from age. Though he slowed down as he passed each house, I knew he would stop when he reached ours: a modest three-bedroom, one-bath Craftsman with a detached garage that my parents bought in 1922, the year my sister Jane was born. It sat on the corner of East Washington and Locust streets in Boise, Idaho.

My mother was Wong's best customer; he often said so. He rolled up the curtain on his truck. The vegetables were nicely displayed: turnips, parsnips, carrots, radishes, dry onions, rutabagas, squash, and more. Jane and I grew up eating plates heaped with Wong's vegetables because Mother had studied dietetics at Brigham Young University in Utah and was convinced that eating "fresh" was the answer to good health long before the rest of the world had given it a thought.

It was January 1932, the Year of the Monkey, and the Chinese New Year was in progress. The celebration started at the turn of the Chinese lunar calendar, with the first new moon, and ended with the Lantern Festival on the night of the full moon. It lasted fifteen days and was a celebration to honor their ancestors.

Today Wong brought us gifts as he celebrated: lychee nuts, candied ginger and a beautiful bright pink silk handkerchief embroidered with lotus blossoms. Wong was the one who awakened my interest in Chinese people, their culture and their food.

My mother was amazed that he took such a liking to me as the Chinese were notorious for favoring boys.

"You were born in the Year of the Tiger," he told me. "That is good." He didn't explain why. I would have to ask him the next time he came because he carried a basket of vegetables into our kitchen and was gone.

It was years later that I discovered why Wong thought being born in the Year of the Tiger was a good thing. If you are a tiger, you will be sensitive, emotional, forthright, adventurous, a problem solver, a leader, courageous, imaginative, and true to your word. Wow! That gave me a lot to live up to.

My father was an attorney—a man of impeccable ethics. He walked in the footsteps of his father who had been an attorney in Grant City, Missouri, where Daddy was born. His father became the prosecuting attorney before he brought his family west. My father's formal education stopped after the fourth grade, yet he was self-taught and managed to pass the bar examination. He went into private practice in the law firm of Oppenheim and Lambert, then went on to hold important posts such as Assistant Idaho Attorney General and Adjudicator for the State Insurance Fund.

He loved to read, especially the Greek philosophers. He told me that Aristotle had written on many subjects and was likely the smartest man that ever lived. Daddy was most interested in Aristotle's dissertations on metaphysics, the virtues and ethics. He also read <u>Time</u> magazine and the <u>Congressional Record</u> to keep up on world events and he enjoyed the <u>Saturday Evening Post</u> every week.

Before I was school age he entertained me with <u>Alice in Wonderland</u>, <u>Through the Looking Glass</u>, <u>Tom Sawyer</u> and the <u>Arabian Nights</u> and more. After he had filled me with all that wonder, I often told him stories and he would write them down on a steno pad in shorthand or type them into his Underwood.

By the time I was thirteen, my daddy had developed asthma and his doctor told him the best thing he could do for himself was walk. When the weather was mild, I would walk with him. We often went up Warm Springs Avenue to the Natatorium and then back down the avenue to the Chinese district downtown, where we most always had a bowl of noodles at Shanghi-lo's. On those walks I learned about the virtues. It was hard to wrap my mind around those ideas, but it was a beginning. My dad was like a walking encyclopedia and I hung on to every word. He was a handsome man; my girl friends thought he looked like Charles Boyer, the movie star.

My mother took care of the necessities of life. She was no nonsense, a tough disciplinarian and an excellent cook. Her remedy for most everything was to soak your feet in Epsom salts. She was the first to criticize and the last to praise. She was hard to please, but oh, how I tried.

The best gift my mother ever gave me was her tenacity. She'd often say, "There isn't anything you can't do, if you put your mind to it." I was receptive as a sponge. It was as though those words were emblazoned across my forehead to be mine forever more.

She wasn't satisfied with just being a housewife. In 1919, she worked at the Ada County Courthouse where she met my dad. She followed him and his entourage to a California beach where she competed for his favor – she won. She went to work again during the Great Depression out of necessity as few people were able to pay their attorneys when the going got tough. Daddy mentioned, one day, how sad it was to have his clients cross the street to avoid him because there wasn't money to pay him for his services.

The family, including my grandma, who was living with us, ate at the round table in the dining room every evening where Jane and I were questioned about our day's activities and Daddy would mesmerize us with his tall tales that would last until we had to go to bed.

Although we were in the middle of the Depression, my parents gave both of us girls piano lessons -- which I never mastered -- and dancing lessons which I simply adored. Dancing paired with my whimsical nature, my relish for drama. My Grandpa Thompson wanted to take me to Hollywood but my parents scoffed at the idea.

When I was a teenager, I was poking around my dad's typewriter where I found an unfinished letter to his cousin Elizabeth Locke who still lived in Grant City, Missouri. She was a poet and had some of her work published in the <u>Good Housekeeping</u> magazine. I was in awe of that. Daddy wrote something to the effect that after reading some of my high-school compositions, he thought I had the stuff to be a successful writer. I was delighted with the idea; I didn't know he had such thoughts, or that it was a possibility for me.

But then, I realized my leanings were toward the arts and not the sciences. I thought about how important color was to me, how I loved art, dance and drama, and more than anything, expressing myself with words. How exciting my life ahead could be.

During two years at Boise Junior College, I became the choreographer for the Follies, a reporter for the college newspaper, and wrote a school column for the Idaho Statesman, which I had been doing since junior high. That was how Betty Penson became my mentor.

Most importantly, I had fallen in love with Jack McLeod who had just come back from the war. It was kismet. Jack had been in the service for five years; our ages were five years apart. If the numbers hadn't jibed like that, we probably wouldn't have met. Jack became the core of my existence.

With all my extra-curricular activities, my grades plummeted. It was a shock as I had sailed through high school with good grades. Nonetheless, not easily dissuaded, I sought out a university that taught creative writing. The only one I found in the Northwest was the University of Oregon.

Mrs. Hershey, our college registrar, told me I'd never be accepted by Oregon, as my grades were too low. "You'd have to get straight A's in sixteen credits in summer school and that's pretty much of an impossibility."

"I can do that," I replied. I had to prove her wrong. I took twelve credits in American literature and four in botany that summer and scored all A's; I was ready for the University of Oregon.

Dr. Eugene Chaffee, president of Boise Junior College, had just returned from the war. He called me into his office and told me he was delighted with my choreography for the Follies, and my mime of Betty Hutton where I did a rendition of her singing, "Doing It The Hard Way."

"I always thought you were just a flapper; I had no idea you had such talent. After you finish your education, there's a job waiting for you on my staff if you want it," he said. I was flattered and liked the idea but it never happened because I didn't go back to Boise for seven years and when I did, I had my hands full raising three boys.

Lois Chaffee, President Chaffee's wife, religiously sent me clippings from the <u>Idaho Statesman</u> when something I had done appeared in the newspaper. I wrote a book of haiku: *The Gift*, and then a novel: *Out of In-*

nocence, that the <u>Statesman</u> covered, but most of the clippings were real-estate related. I think the Chaffees had special interest in me because my mother was instrumental in raising funds for the college in its infancy and they became friends.

After all the effort it took to get to the University of Oregon, I was disappointed. I learned the registrar at Oregon, Mr. Avery, was also the creative writing teacher and not at all what I expected. I was troubled when he said, "With all the veterans coming back to school, girls have no business taking up desks in classrooms. You'll all just get married anyway."

Mr. Avery was colorless; I remember him as a ho-hum sort of instructor. I was disappointed, but I was there and I'd make the best of it.

I enrolled in journalism and drama classes, but found my niche in English literature. I adored Dr. Mundle, a Scot, who made Homer come alive, and Dr. Lesh who taught Shakespeare. Lesh was a temperamental man, who got migraine headaches. He threw erasers at students who nodded off in his class. Now, <u>he</u> was colorful. My class with Dr. Lesh started at eight o'clock in the morning and the Kappa Gammas, whose house was several blocks up the hill from Deade Hall, were always late. One morning, Dr. Lesh was reading from <u>Othello</u> just as the Kappa Gammas rushed into the subterranean room interrupting the class, as he read the stage direction: *"Enter the three whores from Baghdad."* Needless to say, the Kappa Gammas were never tardy again.

I got sick in the middle of the entrance exam and couldn't finish it, which resulted in a low score. It came to light when Dr. Lesh reviewed my essay on Olivia's obsession in Twelfth Night and told me it wasn't congruent with my entrance test. "Who wrote this? It's an excellent piece. Comparing it your entrance exam score, I don't think you did," he said.

"I wrote it," I protested. "But I got queasy in the middle of the entrance exam and couldn't finish. I tried to talk to the professor monitoring the room and he just shrugged and took my papers. There wasn't anything I could do but leave."

"Well," he said, as his face softened, "that explains it. If you want me to, I can arrange to have you take that test again."

"Oh, yes, indeed, I do," I answered. That was a load off my mind. Even if wouldn't affect my grades, it was a matter of pride.

Mrs. Ernest, who taught versification, was happy with my first real poetic efforts. Little did she know I was just writing love poems to Jack. She encouraged me at a time I really needed it: I had come to Oregon to learn to write, only to learn that what was offered was nothing like I expected.

I enrolled in a class called "The Syllogisms of Reasoning" and another called "Ethics," that had a big impact on me. Those classes were so reminiscent of the times I spent with my dad, that I mailed the textbooks home to him after I finished the courses along with a big book I found at the bookstore about Aristotle.

Jack finished his second year at Boise Junior College and followed me to Oregon, where he studied math and philosophy. I remember moving a barrier and driving a borrowed car over McKenzie Pass, which was closed because of the deep snow, to pick Jack up in Bend, Oregon. After Jack admonished me for taking such a risk, he called the Forest Service to find Willamette Pass was open. We went back to Eugene that way.

I graduated in June. Jack and I were married in the Presbyterian Church on the twenty-ninth of August, 1948. We had the perfect honeymoon on Payette Lake even though Jack twisted his ankle showing me how virile he was by running on a log in the lake that was riddled with knotholes. I was impressed just like he knew I would be; he was my hero. However, he spent the rest of our honeymoon soaking his foot in Epsom salts.

After we tried out every one of the seven beds in our cabin at Bowling Green Cottages, creating a ton of laundry for Mrs. Bowling, (I couldn't believe we did that), I went back to Oregon with Jack so he could finish his senior year.

Jack bought an old jalopy: a 1936 Plymouth dubbed the Blue Beetle. When it rained, which it did incessantly, the windshield leaked buckets. We couldn't afford to have it fixed so after trying unsuccessfully to patch it with chewing gum and scotch tape, we threw a piece of plastic over our legs when we drove on rainy days, which was most of the time.

We lived off campus in a makeshift apartment that had once been the upstairs bedrooms. The icebox was on the landing, halfway down the stairway and twenty-two steps from the kitchen. Mr. Tucker, our landlord, had explained that the last renters had flooded the downstairs by not emptying the melted ice so he moved it where it could drain on an outside wall. Somehow, that didn't bother me. What bothered me was that our apartment oozed with the acrid stench of cabbage as it wafted up from Mrs. Tucker's kitchen most every day.

I went to work for the Oregon Newspaper Publisher Association. Carl Webb, my boss, was very patient with me as I learned his business. He was a brilliant man and especially kind.

Because of the change in Jack's marital status, his GI check was held up for a month and there would be no paycheck for me until I had earned one. So we lived on a case of peas that we bought for seven cents a can. When we couldn't bring ourselves to eat one more pea, we showed up at Jack's friend's house. It was dinner time and Freddy Yahn and his wife Ann urged us to join them, just like we hoped they would. After doing a reasonable amount of protesting, we stayed.

Jack's math buddies showed up late one night and got Jack out of bed. I put a pillow over my head and tried to go back to sleep. Jack came in and asked me if I would make waffles. That got me out of bed. It rained incessantly in Eugene and it was common to find that weevils had invaded the flour even on the grocery shelves, but I was too much asleep and a little put out with Jack's buddies to deal with it properly. As long as I live, I will never forget the awful thing I did. As I stirred the waffle batter, I flipped weevils into the trash, one after another. I found three of them. I made the waffles and went back to bed. The next morning Jack thanked me and told me the waffles were delicious. I couldn't bring myself to tell him what I had done. It was a secret I vowed to take with me to my grave; but now I've let the cat out of the bag.

Jack graduated, and found a job with the Bureau of Reclamation in Montana on the Hungry Horse Dam Project. Before we left Oregon, we rolled the Blue Beetle on the Santyan Pass in a snowstorm. After we were rescued from the accident, we spent the night in the only hotel in Sweet Home, Oregon. It sat over a bar. The jukebox was so loud it made it difficult to get to sleep, as over and over it played, *"AS THE GREAT BIG SAW CAME NEARER AND NEARER AND NEARER TO VERA."* Our bed creaked half the night because I got the shakes as an aftermath of our accident.

Because our car was beyond repair, my parents borrowed a little trailer to hold our possessions. They hitched it behind their car and delivered us to Hungry Horse where we lived for months with no transportation. We carried our groceries up the hill from theGeneral-Shea-Morrison's Quonset hut grocery, rain or shine. But we had each other so nothing else really mattered. We loved the great outdoors, and northern Montana was nature's wonderland. Everything came in giant proportions: the mountains, the lakes, the sky. Even the huckleberries were as big as cherries.

We lived only a few miles from Glacier National Park. What a romantic place to start our lives together. We spent five years there watching the Hungry Horse Dam take shape and that's where our first son, John, was born.

How lucky we were. Jack managed to get reassigned to Boise after the dam was complete. Our parents were aging and we wanted John to know his grandparents.

My parents gave us a building lot on a hillside in the east end of town and Jack had his first experience designing a house. It had a low-pitched gabled roof with lots of overhang, walls of window, a big fireplace, and beamed ceiling. It was unique in Boise and had been inspired by Frank Lloyd Wright. We financed it on the GI Bill that didn't require a down-payment. It appraised at $13,500. Jess Hatcher and Rudy Javernick fell heir to a barrel of nails which were hard to come by after the war, and that was the deciding factor in their going into the building business. They contracted our house. We painted and stained the exterior and interior ourselves to lessen the cost. People would come by and we would give them the tour but then we realized we hadn't done much painting. So as the stream of inquisitive people continued to invade the house, Jack told them when they asked all kinds of questions, "Oh, we're just the painters." John was three and Tom was almost a year old when we moved in: 1954. Kevin came along seven years later.

Landscaping our hillside home fell on my shoulders. It was totally new to me since I knew zip about gardening. Fortunately, Jack's dad, who was Boise Park Commissoner, came to my rescue and helped me out. One day I was frustrated because the job seemed unending and my muscles were aching. "Adelaide," he said in his Scottish brogue, "you need to learn patience." I took that to heart.

One of the many nice things about being married to Jack McLeod was being exposed to his creativity as some of it rubbed off on me. The home he designed was avant-garde and the talk of the town in conservative Boise. It would become the springboard for our family persona. Together, we discovered a world of new ideas and we delved into architecture, not knowing at the time that our sons would one day "rub against the old stone" to become creative in their own ways. The excitement in our family seemed to evolve around some form of construction. Where Jack designed the structure and shape, I would do the decorating. We worked well together, each contributing to the other. Those were the best of times.

Color was very important in my surroundings, in my dress and in my garden. Through time, I developed a knack for it and I'm still on call when someone needs suggestions when choosing which colors to paint a wall or a house. I knew it was admirable to stay true to a period or style in decorating but my fun began when I could go eclectic and successfully stir the pot into something excitingly new.

I did the mandatory things that mothers do, such as PTA, and Cub Scouts and organized women for dance and exercise. We called our group, "The Old Bags Ballet." Four years in a row, Ann Wyatt and I chaired Stunt Night and won top honors. Each grade school participated with a seven-minute skit. It was a challenge because of the time restriction. Our scenery, made of cardboard boxes and painted bright colors, looked amazingly professional and we were accused of having outside help.

Jack and I raised our three boys in that East End house and it couldn't have been nicer.

The foothills were only a block away and Roosevelt School was four. The boys had so much freedom exploring the open countryside. They were smart and bright-eyed and grew up with straight, firm bodies and good health. What more could a mother ask?

The day came when the boys were beginning to leave the nest and I wondered just what was I going to do with my life. I was totally convinced that you can only play so much bridge before your brain shrivels.

The Fascinating World of Real Estate

If you stay at a thing long enough it gets under your skin and becomes part of you like the freckles on your nose, and you can't do a thing about it. That is how it was with me and the real-estate business.

In the spring of 1970, without much warning, I found myself ensconced in real estate. My mother started her real-estate career as a broker when she was seventy. She developed a subdivision, bought and sold ranches, helped her Warm Springs Avenue widow friends shed their mansions that were eating them alive with taxes and maintenance, and she even scored a big commercial sale with Opel Harvester, over the bridge table. So you see the apple didn't fall far from the tree.

But the idea of going into real estate didn't remotely excite me. I dragged my feet every step of the way; I was still intrigued with the idea of becoming a writer. My father had passed on by then and that was all the more reason to write. He had a dream for me and more than anything, I wanted to make that dream come true.

But, my mother's legs were failing her and she needed someone with good knees to climb the stairs. Well, I had them. I made the detour, and did what I could to help her. The rest is history. Once I got the hang of it, I realized real estate fit me like spandex. I liked working in real estate -- no, I loved it. It became my passion, and to think: people were paying me to do it.

Shortly after I got my real-estate license, my mother took off for California to visit my sister Jane, which left me running the shop. The phone rang off the hook and I found myself putting my first transaction together. It was nothing short of a nightmare but somehow with numerous phone calls to California, I muddled through and sold a house to Dick and Ann Vycital. Dick was a doctor looking for rental property close to St. Luke's Hospital as an investment, and we had a house in our inventory that fit the bill. I'm not sure if the Vycitals realized that was my first sale, but I wasn't about to tell them. In the course of events, the McLeods and the Vycitals became friends and spent many glorious days together on the ski hill. Making money is nice and the consequence of working smart, but there are a lot of other paybacks in our business.

In 1973, my mother went back to her bridge game and suggested I get my broker's license. I did and supported the company by managing a handful of rental properties belonging to Dr. Beeman. The library in our home became my office, but in no time I learned it wasn't fun to be caught in my bathrobe when clients popped in before eight in the morning, which they were inclined to do.

Being the cautious sort, I migrated to a small corner in the Bush Mansion on Franklin Street, directly behind Boise High School. I wound up saving the building from the wrecking bar. The Methodist Church bought it to tear it down as they desperately needed the land for a parking lot. I approached them, explaining that there were few Gothic Victorian houses of that caliber in Boise. The Bush Mansion was second only to the Cunningham Estate, on the corner of Warm Springs Avenue and Walnut Street. After due consideration, the church graciously agreed that the Bush Mansion should be preserved and asked me to market it and make that happen.

I toured the building with one of my first agents, Margaret Burpee, her friend Florence Martz, and Florence's son Glen, in tow. Glen was a young architect just home from an Ivy League college. He bought the building with the idea of refurbishing it. Shortly thereafter, I moved in.

My space was so small that people waiting to see me sat on the lower steps of the back staircase. Some days, saws, sanders, drills and vacuums ran all day. When the noise became intolerable, we would retreat to Jim's Coffee Shop, on Fort Street, to conduct business. About the time the refurbishing was finished on the first and second floors, my income had grown and I moved to larger digs on the second floor. Dr. Wallace Pond, a psychologist, took the space I had abandoned and we became friends.

He was fussing over the McFall Hotel he owned in Shoshone, Idaho. Built during the railroad construction days early in the twentieth century, it sat just steps from the train track that went through the middle of town. The winters were killing Wally because of the humongous heat bills. He had to keep the building heated as he had a few regulars who called it home.

When a tenant left, Wally could count on the fact that everything detachable would go with him including the toilet paper. His logic told him it was better to have some income than nothing at all.

He was moaning about the hotel over lunch, one day, when it occurred to him that he should sell it. Quite naturally, he looked to me. I didn't know a blessed thing about Shoshone; I usually slept through it when we drove to ski Sun Valley. But Wally was in pain and there was nothing I could do short of listing the hotel. It would be a longshot as there isn't much call for dilapidated albatrosses in one of Idaho's almost-ghost towns. Who would want it and what for? But hope springs eternal and I set out to find a buyer. Lo and behold, a man came out of the woodwork and yes, he could see the potential, it suited him just right. I didn't argue. Wally was pleased; he thought I had created a miracle.

Some time later, Wally married Barbara. They decided they should live in her house and rent his. The quiet of an early morning was broken by the roar of a chainsaw.

Wally looked out the window to see the man who owned the rental house next door carrying a chainsaw like it was a machine gun, leaving devastation in his wake. He had destroyed a portion of the fence that separated Pond's property from his and hacked down a tree that he left sprawling on the ground.

A property-line dispute had erupted when the owner decided to sell his rental. The fence had been built in the 1950s by a previous neighbor and now, the possible buyer of the house demanded that the five-foot strip of land that had been considered part of Pond's property all those years be included in the purchase. Sitting on the land in question were huge pine trees, Barbara's perennial garden and a dog run.

Wally, the savior of lost souls, went fearlessly into the backyard to determine what had driven this man to such anger. The chainsaw was pointed in his direction in a menacing way. Yelling over the noise, Wally finally convinced the man to turn the thing off.

"This dirt belongs to me," the man growled. "I own the ground you are standing on."

He started to fire up his chainsaw again while Wally wondered how he could defuse a guy who was like a Roman candle just begging to be lit.

"Well," Wally said in his controlled voice, "I think we should talk to our attorneys and see what can be done."

"I already have."

"Give me a little slack; I'll call my attorney today. Help me out here," Wally pleaded.

The neighbor hesitated. "You better be quick about it because I'm going to rip down the rest of the fence. I may have a buyer and I want this cleared up," the man said.

About $7,000 later, the attorney hadn't been able to solve the problem. Wally stood over my desk as he mumbled, "I need a miracle. Have I come to the right place?"

With such belief in my prowess, I somehow had to find a solution. After a sleepless night, I decided I had better buy the neighbor's house before he sold it to someone else. That would protect the Ponds' property. I approached the neighbor with cash on-the-line. He was amenable and we struck a deal. Becoming the property owner left me free to quit claim the chunk of land in question to the Ponds. As I planned to put the house on the market, I gave it a little facelift. A few embellishments kept the house from looking Plain Jane and it was fun doing it. I didn't lose a dime on the venture. What a kick! I felt good all over.

One day, two builders and their wives came to the office all in separate cars. It was raining and they were disgruntled because they had to park blocks away and walk through a storm.

The lack of parking was exacerbated by the Boise High School students as every darn one of them seemed to have a car. The problem was incurable and that motivated me to look for larger quarters with adequate parking.

I have always had incredible luck. Things just seem to come my way. I found the perfect building three blocks down Franklin Street. Margaret had heard that people by the name of Wylie were thinking of selling the Hal Coffin House they had lived in for years, and moving to something smaller now that their nine children were raised. They hadn't put their home on the market yet, and while Connie, the owner, knew they needed to sell, she was having withdrawal jitters. She was afraid some buyer would cut up her cherished home of many years into ugly little apartments, and that would break her heart.

The house was perfect: circa 1904, a brick and sandstone Georgian, with an impressive wide, oak front door, southern maple woodwork, leaded-glass windows, high ceilings, four sets of double doors, a masterful floor plan and best of all it had escaped the 1960s remodeling frenzy that swept through Boise with devastating effects. It was built for Hal Coffin, state treasurer, and his bride. The Coffins eventually sold it to a German lady who was a fantastic cook. She board and roomed young professional men. Serving them delectable food on white linen tablecloths, the German lady became legendary and to get on the list of her tenants was a real coup. What fun it would be to sell real estate while housed in a building with such rich history.

Heavy draperies covered the leaded windows. A 1904 <u>Capitol News</u> article chronicling the building said that the windows were cut in Italy and leaded in France. In reading the rest of the article it was clear there had been little change through the years; the house was like an untouched jewel. Connie pulled the drapery away from the window, and I got a quick glimpse half-hidden by murky plastic. The window defied all superlative adjectives: it was an elegant floral design. Then, the window was quickly covered again. I wanted to see the upstairs, but that didn't happen: Connie was too nervous. I knew I was walking on eggs so I didn't press her for further viewing.

Imagine a Realtor buying a building without seeing the upstairs or the basement. Ridiculous! I was a classic example of an overly emotional buyer. I couldn't help it. I told her I loved it, it was perfect and I wouldn't compromise it with ill-designed remodeling, and that I would cherish it as she had.

I stopped to admire a lovely bronze sculpture, an elegant piece of art, on the newel post at the bottom of the oak stairway: a fanciful, barefoot, curvaceous maiden with a wreath of flowers in her hair. Connie was quick to tell me it was not included in the sale; she would take it with her. As negative as that might sound, it made me think she was going to sell her house to me. She did.

The day we closed, after all the documents were signed, she left my office and then scurried back to tell me she would leave the bronze. Knowing I would have it was exciting, but more important, that told me she was satisfied with the transaction.

I wasn't as nice as she was. Thirty-one years later when I reluctantly sold the building, I took the sculpture with me. I desperately needed a souvenir.

When I had the building appraised for insurance, the agent's wife, an antique dealer, pointed out that the bronze was French and signed by the artist Augustus Moreau and titled *Messagere du Printemp* (<u>Messenger of Spring</u>). A tiny imbedded medallion plaque verified its authenticity. After the antique dealer told me what the bronze was worth, I was tempted to bring my sleeping bag down to the office to guard it through the nights.

During the month of December, we almost forgot Christmas and concentrated on getting the building ready to occupy by the first of January. If it hadn't been for Jack and son John, I doubt I could have pulled it off. It was a madhouse. At times, there were as many as twenty workmen getting in each other's way: tending to the complex telephone system; maple floor refinishing; getting the electric up to snuff; a new roof; and fresh wallpaper and paint. The southern pine woodwork had been so well cared for through the years that it almost looked like new.

Jack and I met an electrician at the building one evening. The hall light upstairs wasn't working and we wanted him to fix it. He took off the antique brass cover plate and placed it on the stair railing. After looking the job over, he went to his shop to get some parts. While he was gone, there was nothing we could do and being dead tired, we looked for someplace to relax and each of us found a chair in a different room. The quiet was interrupted by someone stirring around upstairs so I bounced out of my chair thinking it was Jack. But he was still resting his eyes. When our electrician returned, he complained that the brass plate he had carefully left on the railing had disappeared. After thoroughly searching for the missing plate, I told the electrician that I had heard a noise upstairs while he was gone.

His eyes grew wild. "A ghost! You've got yourself a ghost. I'm not going back up there," he whispered as he slithered out the door. Jack and I had a good laugh over that and went home to bed.

The next day, Jack discovered the brass plate sitting on the stair railing just where the electrician had left it. Through the years, there were lots of times someone heard noises at night. We found squirrels living in our attic. That was all it was ... well, maybe.

When we unveiled the leaded-glass windows, we were in awe. We found the original chandeliers nicely wrapped and boxed in the attic, along with extra stair rungs and miscellaneous woodwork. We reinstalled the lights where we thought they had originally been. And just imagine, we discovered the light switches under layers of wallpaper and they still worked.

I had to convert the zoning from residential to L-O (Limited Office) which turned out to be no small task because I was one of the first in Boise to do so. It required a hearing with Planning and Zoning. Their reception was dicey but in the end I got the job done.

Jack designed a delightful octagon-shaped conference room that opened to the garden, allowing us to abandon the creepy basement where we held our weekly meetings. We had a leak in the roof over the back porch so it was better to build a sun-room above it rather than patch the hole. The room faced south and required some sort of protection on hot summer days. The Pioneer Tent and Awning Company built a twenty-foot-long automatic awning. If the sun was bright, it rolled out; if it was windy enough to cause damage to the awning, or if the sun disappeared, it rolled in.

Before we were content, we took in the side porch, enlarged it and made an elegant office space. The additions were well crafted and in the spirit of the existing building and with the proper materials including the vintage egg and arrow trim boards; if you weren't privy to what was new and what wasn't, you'd be hard-pressed to detect the additions from the original. Jack was a genius.

Watch Out Below

Our first spring, we enhanced the garden with new landscaping including a rose garden. Jack and son Kevin built a beautiful sandstone wall which matched the stone on the house, to give us privacy. It curved to accommodate a large silver maple tree, the tallest tree in the neighborhood. I can remember Jack saying, "This wall will be here long after I'm gone." Just weeks later, we had a horrific windstorm and the maple fell, decimating the wall, Jean Smith's Volvo and my Mercedes.

Carole Gill, who had first-hand knowledge of such storms, gathered up everybody in the building and took them to the basement. I was at the Powells' next door, our neighborhood photographer, as Alice Powell and I were arranging a venue for the Altruists Club in my garden. I got up from my chair to leave. I don't know why, but I lingered and not much more than a minute later, the tree crashed to the ground. If I had left when I first intended to, I would have been a grease spot on the sidewalk.

It was amazing and gratifying that so many guys with chainsaws showed up and cleaned up the debris in jig time. That triggered a "thank you" party for them.

It was time to create a logo for the company. What would look good on signs and in newspaper advertising? With the name McLeod, I was entitled to use the McLeod tartan: a garish egg-yolk yellow field, with black and red crisscrossing through it. The colors *would* draw attention on a yard sign, although I never thought they were especially pleasing. Making that move set the stage for hiring a bagpiper for special occasions.

One morning, while I was still honing the look I wanted for my logo, a vintage panel truck stopped in front of our building and a young man named Noel Weber came into the office. He was a graphic artist, a very good one, I decided after looking at his portfolio. He was new to Boise and anxious to design our logo. I was agreeable. He created a striking design I would use as long as I was in business. He made a piece of art out of our company name -- McLeod Realty -- written in stunning Victorian script. It was perfect and exuded a sense of elegance. With a swath of McLeod tartan that went diagonally across our yard signs, we used Noel's artwork in the middle to complete our logo and we also used it in our advertising, and on our business cards.

Later, he reproduced the design on glass and won top honors in an international graphic arts competition. It was gorgeous; I bought it once the competition was over.

After we had been in business for years, I felt it was time to update our image and I decided to introduce our other tartan just because I liked the colors better. It was blue and green with touches of red, yellow and black. The change might give new life to the company. I didn't want our advertising to become stale; changing the tartan would freshen things up. What I didn't consider was that I was doing away with an image that had given us stature and had become familiar. But there was no going back because 250 signs using the new tartan had been delivered.

While I was still a neophyte in real estate, I got a phone call on a house I had listed in the North End. The voice was strangely off-key and raspy. He wanted to see the house, but had no transportation. He asked me to pick him up downtown. I agreed to meet him in front of St. Michael's Cathedral at Eighth and State Streets. After I hung up, I had second thoughts. The man's voice had been very peculiar and I didn't know a blasted thing about him. While I was driving there, I decided, if I didn't like his looks, I wouldn't stop. I soon discovered he was a young Chinese immigrant named Kim Lo. He wasn't alone. His wife and tiny doll-like daughter stood beside him. You can imagine my relief.

We overcame the language barrier with the help of charades and once we toured the house, he wanted to make an offer. I was hesitant because I wondered if Kim could make the payments on his salary. I went to the Twin Dragon restaurant where he worked as a cook. The manager convinced me that the Chinese live on a lot less than Americans do and if there was a problem, Kim Lo would have the support of the Chinese community. I was satisfied.

After all the documents were signed and mailed to my seller, the attorney involved decided he wanted to anglicize the buyer's name. Did the attorney have the right to change a person's name after it had been his identity all of his life? I didn't think so, but there was nothing I could do about it. What he did was turn the names around as Kim was his surname and Lo was his given name. It was just the opposite from the way we compile names in America. This entailed sending out new documents. My seller was an elderly lady who had gone to California to live with her daughter and was facing surgery that she might not survive. I quickly mailed the new documents and the lady signed them just before she died. Kim and his wife raised their daughter in that little house and as far as I know, they are still living there.

The Agents

Kathy Jones, a pretty brunette with wildly expressive brown eyes and a winning smile, had just joined our company. She drove a red Cadillac with a white roof that was about a block long. She decided it wasn't the image she wanted to portray so she put an ad in the <u>Idaho Statesman</u> to sell it. She would buy a smaller car, one not so flashy.

It wasn't long before an enormous black man arrived at our door, dressed to the nines in a maroon satin jacket and a ton of jewelry around his neck and on his hands. His grooming was immaculate.

The receptionist summoned Kathy to the foyer where we greeted people, and Kathy's eyes popped out of her head when she saw him. Right there, in front of everybody, he opened his wallet and peeled out a good number of hundred dollar bills, handing them to Kathy one at a time. Kathy flushed, grabbed the loot, gave the man the title and the keys to the car and vanished back up the stairs leaving folks wondering just what was going on.

Janet Kell, a clever energetic young woman, heard that we were hiring a receptionist and called and told me not to give the job to anyone else; she wanted it. I knew Janet from McCall where her parents summered next door to our cabin in Pilgrim Cove. In fact, I had been their Realtor when they bought their place. I hired Janet and in no time she was telling agents which of our listings they should show their customers. She was usually right on target. I could see she had talent that was being wasted and although she was a dandy receptionist, I suggested she get her real-estate license and she became a highly successful agent. Her father, Keith Gilmore, was a retired Realtor and a land investor and I'm pretty sure she received guidance from him. One time, Janet sold a house and the seller was in the process of moving out when she found that the buyers were flaking.

"What should I do?" she asked me.

"You will just have to find another buyer," I said. And wouldn't you know it, before the day was over she had a new buyer in place.

I loved the confidence Naomi Farber showed when she came to interview at the office. The first thing out of her mouth was, "You need me." She was a pretty lady and always immaculately dressed, so I knew something had gone awry when she stumbled into the office, carrying her high-heeled shoes, one in each hand, looking like she'd gone through a wringer and been tromped on. She was so furious, she was shaking.

Gasping for breath, she told me. "I was at a meeting at a downtown hotel and as I glanced out a window that overlooked the parking lot, I saw my Mercedes in the process of being hauled away. I ran out screaming at the tow-truck driver who by that time had my car strapped up and was beginning to move. I chased after it, yelling at the driver when I could get my breath. He stopped at a red light and I caught up and jumped in the driver's seat of my car where I honked the horn trying to get the guy's attention. He kept moving and I kept honking. He finally pulled over and stopped," she said, as she swept a wisp of hair from her eyes. "He came back and told me I was parked in a no parking zone and it was his job to haul my car away.

I told him, "You can't do that. It's my car. I'll call the police."

"There's a pay phone right over there. Go ahead call the police," he said.

"Dodging traffic, I finally reached the pay phone and turned around to catch a glimpse of the tow-guy driving away."

Naomi's saga was like a cartoon playing in my head and I wanted to laugh but I was afraid that she wouldn't see the humor in it right then.

Naomi told us at our Tuesday meeting, "I have a possible listing to tour on Whitehead, off of Hill Road. I'd like you all to help me price it. I don't have the exact address but Whitehead is a short street and it is the nicest house."

My carload of agents turned down Whitehead, and there was a house that fit Naomi's description. This must be it.

It was our unwritten code that we always waited for the listing agent before entering a house, but this was that proverbial cold day in January and we were freezing. We rang the doorbell and no one answered. We tried the knob and the house wasn't locked so we went inside. Dishes were stacked in the sink and the beds were unmade so we decided to do Naomi a favor and tidy up.

When Naomi came down the road in her green Mercedes, she drove on by. She stopped in front a stand of trees and bushes that hid a house that was built way back on its lot. We hadn't noticed it. That was Naomi's listing.

Come to find out, the Robinettes owned the house we had invaded. She is a Realtor so we hoped she would understand and get a laugh out of it. If not, at least, she didn't have to do the dishes or make the beds when she got home.

Later, I received a telephone call from my friends on the board of the Methodist Church. They asked if I was interested in doing some land acquisition for them because they still needed parking.

"I'll get on it right away," I told them. I researched the property within close proximity to discover that Mrs. Carlton, an antique dealer who lived in the neighborhood, owned an old house that had been cut up into apartments, across from the church. I called on her. She was an irascible lady in her seventies.

"Yes, I'd sell, but not unless the price is right. I don't give a darn whether I sell it or not," she said.

"Well, I can't speak for my clients, of course, but I feel you would get a fair price as there is motivation," I said. "It won't do any harm to show it to them."

"Do I have to change my clothes?"

"That's up to you."

I called the Methodist Church and the Board had convened in anticipation. They met Mrs. Carlton and me in front of her rental.

As we went up the walk together, a women in slacks had something dragging out of leg of her pants. Ted Hardy, one of the Board members, deliberately stepped on it and out flew a pair of panty hose. Ted held them up and waved them. It seemed that the lady had taken her slacks and panty hose off together the last time she wore the slacks and that morning when she dressed, she'd forgotten about the panty hose. The woman was embarrassed but took it in stride and laughed so we all did. That was how our day started, and from there on, things got really weird.

Mrs. Carlton led us inside and up a flight of stairs where she rapped on the door just seconds before she put her key in the lock and opened it. A naked young man, half-in and half-out of a sleeping bag, was lying on the floor. He woke with a start, and ran from the room holding the sleeping bag in front of his naked body.

After viewing the dining room and kitchen, Mrs. Carlton threw a door open as she said, "This is the bathroom." And there was that poor kid sitting on the pot.

Back at Mrs. Carlton's house, she and I discussed the deal. "The buyers asked that you give them a price you would accept and they would try to meet it," I said.

We sat at the kitchen table where Mrs. Carlton signed a one-time listing agreement on the property as Carolyn Jones popped in with a bag of groceries. After we greeted each other, Caroline, a Park Point Real Estate agent, told me she was Mrs. Carlton's niece.

Caroline started preparing dinner for Mrs. Carlton. As I walked to the front door with Mrs. Carlton, I whispered to her, "Caroline is in real estate. This must be awkward for you. I didn't know she was your niece. I would understand if you want to include her in this deal."

"Naw! Caroline makes too much money already. She doesn't need my business."

I couldn't see how that could be true. Caroline had come after work, probably dog tired, fixing Mrs. Carlton's dinner. I felt sorry for Caroline, and guilty that I had taken business away that should have been hers. The church accepted the listing price; Mrs. Carlton signed the church's sales agreement, and we closed.

Ann Erstad was looking for a listing in the Highlands; she had a customer who wanted to live there. She found one in our inventory. It was the home of one of our agents and she told Ann: "We'll be out of town but go ahead and show it. Dad lives with us and he'll be there. By the way, he's hard of hearing."

Ann arrived before her customer did and looked through the house so she would be familiar with it in order to enhance her showing. An old man was sitting in a rocking chair in one of the bedrooms. Ann spoke to him but he didn't answer.

Then she remembered that the owner said he was deaf. She touched his shoulder, and though his eyes were open, he still didn't move. He was dead. Ann didn't have time to think as the doorbell was ringing. Desperate times call for desperate measures. She got a blanket and threw it over him, answered the door and showed the house. Although I always admired Ann's ability to make the best of a bad situation, she may have gone a little too far that time.

Margaret, one of my first agents, measured 4' 10" inches tall, if she stood up straight. She was the only one I knew I didn't have to look up to. She made up for her lack in height with her cocky demeanor and her red hair. She was a go-getter. Knowing "everybody" in Boise, as she did, she enjoyed a successful real-estate career. Her husband Bill worked with Jack at the Bureau of Reclamation.

Margaret listed a property on North 15th Street that was in an estate. The house had never been locked which was often the case in the 1970s. She explained to the executor, a farmer from Emmett, who was big as Margaret was small, that when a house is on the market it needs to be locked up. The executor came up with a key and a caveat that if anyone pushed in the auxiliary lock on the front door, there would be no way of getting into the house.

Margaret put a note on the door to that effect, which turned out to be an invitation for some wise guy to do just that. She called the farmer and asked for help. Out of desperation the two of them came up with a plan. The man had a pair of his big overalls in his truck, the kind with straps over the shoulders. They rolled up the legs and Margaret stepped into them. He held on to the straps as he lowered Margaret down the coal chute. Once Margaret was on her feet on the basement floor, she climbed the stairs and unlocked the door from the inside. How I regret I wasn't there to memorialize the event with a photo of Margaret dangling in those overalls.

Jean Smith got up with the sun. Her favorite hangout in the early morning was Denny's Restaurant. In our pajamas and with curlers in our hair, twenty of us descended on Denny's to celebrate Jean's birthday.

Jean's dad, a retired attorney, convinced Jean that she needed to go through the bankruptcy process as a precaution. She was recently divorced and her ex-husband had gone bankrupt. Jean's dad wanted to waylay any possible backlash and he thought this was the best thing for her to do.

So I bought her Volvo for $30, and sold it back to her after the bankruptcy was settled and she filed a homestead on her house. Then, she instigated a Bankrupt Party where we ate beans out of the can and paid ten cents to use the porcelain facility in the bathroom. The ladies came in red, white and blue polka-dot waitress dresses we had found at a thrift store. It was a fun night that we would never forget.

Barb Burnell, a tall attractive blond, met Phil on the internet. Their love affair happened quickly and we knew little about it when she brought Phil and a wedding cake to our Tuesday meeting.

Barb and I had lunch one day at the Piper Pub and she parked her car in the multilevel parking garage. Barb had recently lost her father and was concerned that her mother was losing her memory. Having a bit of a memory problem myself, I felt like an expert on the subject. I told Barb, "It's nothing to worry about. Given her age, your mother has so much stored in her brain that it becomes overly crowded and quite naturally, little pieces of memory fall out from time to time. It isn't Alzheimer's, it's just data overload."

"Do you really believe that?" Barb asked.

"Of course, I have first-hand experience."

"Just the same," Barb said, "I hope my brain doesn't go soft when it comes to remembering things."

When we left the restaurant and went to find Barb's car in the parking garage, she couldn't remember where she had parked it.

Ann Samuelsen was a delight to have around the office. She was always upbeat. Her demeanor seemed to be her protection from all things worrisome. She had a powerful presence when she walked into a room; things seemed to revolve around her -- she was charming.

A group of businessmen wanted to see a triplex on Eighteenth Street that once had been a family home. Ann guided them to the upstairs apartment and the door was open, so they walked in. Sitting on the floor in the middle of the room was a woman in the lotus position obviously practicing yoga. She didn't move a muscle; she was in a trance. The thing was, she was naked to the waist. In that awkward moment, Ann put on her happy face and led the men from the room.

The seventies were the days of FHA loans. It was a tedious procedure. The FHA inspector always seemed to wait for zero hour to make his final inspection. At that point, he would give us heartburn by coming up with a second complicated laundry list of repairs that had to be accomplished before a house could close.

The buyer, in this case, had become weary of the situation. Pat Brush, the seller's agent, knew that if the transaction didn't close by Friday, the bank wouldn't fund, the buyer had threatened to walk and the deal could be off. On Thursday morning, there was still painting to be done before the final inspection scheduled for 4 o'clock that afternoon. Pat hovered over my desk bemoaning the fact that her painter was home with the flu and couldn't finish his job: specifically, the concrete shower walls. Together we went through our list of painters but no one was available on such short notice. We resorted to the telephone book, without success.

As Pat left the office, she mumbled, "I could paint it myself but I don't have time to go all the way up to Dry Creek to change my clothes." A couple of hours later, Pat reappeared with a grin on her face. "Job's done," she giggled.

"How in the world did you manage that?" I wanted to know.

"Simple. I just went to the house, locked the door, pulled the blinds, took off my clothes and painted the shower in the nude."

Women make good Realtors as we are born nurturers and buying or selling real estate can be a stressful endeavor. Women have an attribute missing in most men: we are "long suffering" as we developed patience raising our children.

Gail Jacobs's desk was at the end of the upstairs hall that once had been the maid's quarters. It sat across the hall from a narrow staircase that led down to the kitchen. Her only window was just above the grape arbor that partially blocked her view of the rose garden. Gail decided she would create her own garden. She crawled out the window onto the beams of the arbor, about thirteen feet off the ground, where she nurtured a large pot of morning glories.

Kay Anderson went through a vast amount of training while she was working for Pete O'Neill at River Run Development. Her training taught her to script herself by memorizing verbiage she used when talking to buyers or sellers. She felt it allowed her to keep the conversation on track and maintain control so she could be more productive. Having what she needed to say by rote, there was little margin for error. She also adhered to special language: it was always "townhomes" not townhouses, "a home site" and not a building lot, etc. Her system worked well in getting the best results in hosting open houses. She was a true professional in what she did and how she did it.

It paid off for her. She became top producer in our office. As time went by, some of the our other Realtors, seeing how successful Kay was, tried to emulate her.

Venice Knipe, an attractive and amusing woman, joined our team in the late eighties. One day she came in from a listing call and stood over my desk as she said, "I sold a house to a Chinese woman years ago and she called me this morning because she wanted to sell it."

"How nice. Did you get it listed?" I asked.

"Yes, I did. As I got out of my car in front of the house, she rushed down the steps to greet me. She gave me a big hug and then pushed me away and said, 'Venny, you used to be so pretty, what happened?' " Venice loved to tell stories on herself; it was her thing.

Jean Smith, a/k/a Jeano, was a spark in our office. One of the endearing things about her was how she entertained us with her guitar and made up clever real estate songs she sang to country tunes. Here's the one I liked best:

THE R.E. BLUES
To the tune of Jim Croce's "Car Wash Blues"

I just got out of a training program
Doin' 90 days for Boise Cascade.
Tried to find me an executive position
But no matter how I tried to persuade
They weren't listening to the fact
That I was a genius --
They said, "We got all we can use."
So I got those steadily depressing
Low-down mind messin'
Working in the R. E. blues.

I should be sittin' in an air-conditioned
Limo with a portable bar

Talkin' some trash to the limo-driver:
"Honey, can you drive me far?"

Instead, I'm payin' dues to the Board,
Calling clients on the phone,
And taking all that M.L.S. abuse.
Yeah, I got them steadily depressing,
Low-down mind-messing
Working in the R. E. Blues.

I used to be cool,
Had a salary to count on,
I handled things as quick as they came.
Now, I'm clickin' through the Multiple Listings --
Frankly, my stomach's aflame.
What if my closing flops Tuesday,
My commission dies Wednesday,
And I still owe my Multiple dues?
Yeah, I got those steadily depressing,
Low-down mind messing,
Working in the R. E. blues.

So, please Foxy Adelaide
Have pity upon me,
I'm doin' the best I can do:
Tearing through the Highlands,
Running in the North End,
Trying to make a deal come through;
Sure, I'm using lots of Xerox,
Burning up the phone lines
And pulling off very few coups,
But I got them steadily depressing,
Low-down mind-messing,
Working in the R. E. Blues.

Jean "Raylene" Smith
May 1981

It is hard to pinpoint just what it was about Jeano that made everyone love her. Maybe it was because she was so upbeat and that energized us.

She was the self-appointed clutter police. When the first flower in a bouquet began to fade, it was relegated to the trash bin. We were all appreciative of her effort to keep things spiffed up. She flitted through the office with her dust cloth and dumped anything that was left on the floor. Jeff Orr made the mistake of bringing his IRS worksheets to the office in a grocery bag. He put the bag on the floor beside his desk. Zappppp! It disappeared. Jeff ran to the landfill but it was too late.

She was always right there and handy if there were files to be cleaned out. She finished the job while the rest of us were trying to figure how to go about it. She abhorred meetings that dragged on too long and people who didn't "get it" . . . whatever "it" was.

One time she had to write her biography for a seminar she was taking in Seattle. She took two pages explaining how she was editor of her class newspaper when she was seven years old and then, a short sentence: "I was married and divorced." She had her priorities.

Together, we made a trip to Portland for a seminar, to Los Angeles when we were being courted by Coldwell-Banker, down to see Anne Stringer and Susie and Jeff Orr in southern California, to San Francisco to break in my new Mercedes and, best of all, Hawaii for a real estate convention. We had a great time.

One day Caroline Jones came to see me. "The young bucks at Park Point kicked me out because they think I am too old. Can I work for you?"

I was quick to reply, "Of course you can." I couldn't help remembering what a raw deal she got from her aunt when I was doing the acquisition for the Methodists. Jack and I took Carolyn out to lunch and she was smitten with Jack, just like most of my friends were. The next day she brought in her Rainbird sprinkler and wanted me to take it home and have Jack fix it as it wasn't working just right. When Caroline left my desk, I went out to the garden and hooked the sprinkler to a hose and adjusted it. Then, I put it on Caroline's desk. "I fixed it," I told her.

She got a coy look on her face as she mumbled, "I wanted Jack to fix it."

I can't think of Caroline without smiling. In all the years she was with us, her gracious, dignified presence was capped by her funny bone. She amazed us with her quick retorts; her mind went a mile a minute. There was never a sour word, or a complaint. Even when Caroline fell down the stairs at the office and we all quit breathing, she took it in stride. No bones were broken, but she was bruised and embarrassed. She didn't want anyone's sympathy; it just wasn't her style.

Eventually, Caroline and her custard-colored Audi were getting on in years. One day, I got an urgent call. Caroline was out on the Bench with customers when her Audi died. "Will you come rescue me?" she pleaded.

"I'll be right there," I said. I went with the idea I would drive them home or back to the office, but no: there were other houses that Caroline had not yet shown. It was a hoot chauffeuring them around the rest of the day.

Many of her customers were quick to offer to do the driving when Caroline had set up showings. We all breathed a sigh of relief. She wasn't a high producer but she was constant and had forgotten more about real estate than any of us would ever know and you just had to appreciate her quick wit.

Not only was she pretty, she was well endowed. We were all a little jealous of that. We celebrated her birthday with a party at her son, Bruce's home. We girls stuffed our sweaters with balloons just before Caroline arrived. She walked in the door, and without missing a beat, she laughed as she said, "Well, just look at all the Caroline look-alikes."

When Caroline passed away, it was as though an irreplaceable piece of our puzzle was missing. Her sons asked Maggie Soderberg Simplot and me to do the eulogy. Maggie was an original; I've never known anyone more colorful. She found fun in everything she did. Her whimsy delighted me.

Maggie, in a long black silk coat, talked about how she and Caroline had been such good friends and how she loved her and what Caroline had bequeathed to her, as she opened her coat to reveal two balloons in her sweater. This might seem irreverent but it wasn't. It was just right.

It was my turn. Caroline was a dyed-in-the-wool Democrat and I, a staunch Republican, yet we had a lot in common. We were not only real estate devotees but we both passionately loved our gardens. I remember taking Caroline to Greenhurst Nursery in Nampa. We were so excited with spring that we bought box after box of flowers and only quit when there was no space left in the car.

"Oh," she moaned. "We've lost our heads. How are we going to get all these plants in the ground? We've bought out the nursery." Then she got a far-away look in her eyes as she said, "Oh well, there can't be too much beauty in this world."

Then, I recited a poem I had written with Caroline in mind:

MELANGE MADNESS
My garden is a hodgepodge.
I'm addicted to tucking in one more plant,
Allowing Mother Nature to create her own design,
Relishing each jewel as it unfolds.

Up and down the street there is order,
Trimmed hedges, weeded, prim and proper
A studied balance of evergreen and deciduous,
Bedded in deep bark so weeds can't grow.

But here, the purple beech is allowed to lop guardian
Over tiny danfordii. The cyclamen and sylverstris
Anemones vie for space as they naturalize.
Yesterday, I tucked in a clot of oriental lilies.

Japanese maples grace the shady spots
Where ferns, hostas and begonias flourish.
One must look and look again, not to miss
The pink violets hiding in the grass.

Back from our annual pilgrimage to Greenhurst's
The driveway is lined with boxes of new plants --
If I plant them all, there'll be little room left for weeds.
Saturday, we'll go to Edwards -- if my back permits.

In sunny spots, echinacea and daisies
Hold court in this garden of no rhyme or reason.
Don't you see, I need these treasures to mark
My seasons as surely as I need to breathe.

Drop by this spring to see my garden.
Do come when the iris are in bloom.
Please understand, I'm making no excuses
But, come early, so you can pull a weed or two.

But He Was Such a Nice Guy

David Street, a young man with a gentle demeanor, and a friend of my son, John's, decided he wanted to sell real estate. He was especially likeable and hadn't been in the office long before he made a sale. I was excited for him. Everything went smoothly until the sellers came in the office to close. As David joined us at the conference table, the color drained from his face. He asked me if he could speak to me in the hall. We excused ourselves. "I have never seen those people before," he whispered.

Come to find out, David sold a house in what we called a "California subdivision" where there was a lot of repetition in the design. He had looked in the Multiple Listing book for the house his people wanted to buy and accidentally wrote up a look-alike just one block away.

He gave the document to the listing agent who had the seller sign it. It took some finesse to straighten it out with the "almost sellers," but we managed by explaining what had happened and with a gift card – dinner for two at the Sandpiper Restaurant.

Somewhat later, Dave got a phone call from a man who wanted to see property. Could he pick him up at Grants' Truck Stop? Dave complied. The man wanted to see upper-end homes and Dave took him to the Island at River Run, the ultimate housing development at that time.

The man decided he would like to buy two of the houses they had toured. One was for his mother and the other would be his. Dave wrote the agreements up and the man gave him a good-sized earnest money check. Dave was so excited that he took the man out to dinner at the Gamekeeper Restaurant in the Owyhee Hotel: the best in Boise.

Then, the man asked to be returned to Grants' Truck Stop. The next day when the check was deposited in our trust account, we discovered the check was bogus. The man was a trucker looking for something to do while his truck was being repaired. He got a tour of the city and a wonderful dinner out of it, and Dave got a headache.

Another agent, Doug Kowallis, who was trying to increase his sales, flew with me to San Francisco to solicit business from a third-party company. It had to do with the big companies like Micron, Hewlett-Packard, and Boise Cascade moving their work force around the country. An enterprising person saw a potential in creating a business to facilitate the moves and sold some corporations on his company's services. The corporation involved would advance the funds to move an employee, a real estate company would market his current home, and another real estate company, at the destination, would assist the employee in finding a new home. The third-party company would coordinate the process by organizing the moves, making them happen quickly and smoothly. We were after the part of the business that involved Realtors in Boise.

As we walked into the airport, I asked Doug to get a rental car while I made a phone call. He bounced back within a few minutes to say that his driver's license had expired and he was very sorry. I gave him a half-disgusted grimace and my license. He came back again, this time to tell me my license had also expired. We had a big laugh and hired a taxi for the day to cart us across the bridge to Walnut Creek to do our business.

In the late 1980s, a builder by the name of Vic Johnson came down from Alaska and made a splash in the Boise housing market. He claimed he could build a house in twenty-one days. I was a little skeptical. He met with my son, Tom, and Tom's buyer at a local café. He didn't have an office. The buyers paid for their lot and went to Nevada to put their house on the market. On their return, they drove by their lot and came to the office terribly distraught. Someone had built a house on it.

Baffled, Tom asked them, "Are you sure it's your lot?" Yes, they were sure. Tom called Vic Johnson to tell him what had happened.

Vic laughed as he told Tom, "It's their house. We'll be putting the kitchen in this afternoon and the bathroom in the morning. We will be finished ahead of time. They can move in next Monday."

I couldn't believe what Tom related to me. Vic wasn't the best builder around and he wasn't the worst either. But he sure was the fastest.

I liked having Tom in the office where I could show him the ropes. I worked hard to avoid nepotism that my agents might resent. Tom was in his twenties, fresh out of college where his economics professor told his students that if any of them had parents in business, the smartest move they could make was to get involved. Tom sold starter houses to his friends as they married or established themselves away from their families. It wasn't long before Tom was selling a variety of houses and became a top producer.

After a long time in the real estate business, he had a good handle on what the public was looking for and that led him to design, which eventually became his thrust.

Boise's Annual Rose show was in progress and I wished I had time to go, but there was too much going on at the office. So when Jan O'Neil dropped in and said she had been to the show, I asked for details. "Well," she said, "you should go. I entered a rose and it won."

"What rose did you enter? I asked.

"Well, it's sort of a funny story. I looked my garden over and there wasn't a rose good enough to take so I came down here and found the perfect rose in your garden."

"And . . ."

"I entered it and it won a blue ribbon."

"I don't believe it. Which rose did you take?"

"It was sort of peach blending into yellow. I didn't know its name, so I just gave it one, Peach Parfait."

"You're kidding me, aren't you? No one could get away with that." Jan pulled the blue ribbon out of her handbag. That should have been proof enough, but I couldn't get over the feeling that Jan was putting me on.

When I moved from the Bush Mansion to the Coffin House, I only had seven agents, so I rented the upstairs to the Arts and Humanities Commission. We weren't big enough to employ a regular receptionist, so I talked my youngest son, Kevin, fresh out of high school, into managing the phone calls and taking messages. He was good at it but not crazy about the job. After giving me a year, he told me he wanted to quit and his girlfriend, Kathi wanted the job.

I was hesitant to get wound up in Kev's life that way and told him, "No, I can't do that. It would be more than awkward if you had a falling out with Kathi while she was working for me." But he insisted that I at least give her a chance and I caved in. Kathi had managed a drive-in restaurant down by the college so she came with some managerial know-how. I asked her if she could type, and she said she could learn, so I sent her home with a typewriter to practice. She came back in no time thumping the keys and there was little I could do but hire her. She proved to be a hard worker, and was very mature for her age. I was impressed. My concern was for naught as Kathi and Kevin eventually got married.

At times, our job took us beyond reason into hand-holding, baby-sitting and miracle working. Once in a while, we had buyers who were timid about making a decision. We tried to instill confidence in them as they wavered for hours, afraid to make a commitment. Some clients were inclined to bring their bratty kids with them when they were house hunting. The kids would run amuck and the parents seemed oblivious; it was our job to make sure they didn't touch anything or do any damage. We often had to stretch our brains to find a way to make a transaction happen if a buyer didn't have enough money for a down payment, a blemish on his credit or essential job history. We were well aware that the buyers and sellers were trusting us with their lives; we'd better get it right.

Thankfully, threaded into the earthshaking weightiness of our work came client appreciation and sometimes a little comic relief to preserve our sanity. I was never sure if our gang was unique in the way we saw the funny side of things, or was such levity intrinsic in the real estate business?

From time to time, through the years, it came back to me that our company was used as an example of exemplary ethics in business. There was nothing in my career that made me more proud.

My company seemed to attract the best of people. The criteria for working with us were honesty, good English, intelligence, and it was a plus if you were attractive. A good sense of humor was especially desirable. At first, I didn't like turning applicants down until I realized I was doing them a favor as everyone should be successful at their life's work and some people just weren't cut out for real estate.

When I was new to the business, those days before "head-hunting," real estate brokers honored competitors by not jeopardizing another broker's business. We all were aware, first hand, the hours and effort it took to bring an agent to a productive level. It was taboo to go after another broker's agent. I thought it was not only proper but a classy way to do business.

But sadly that changed. As time went on, every productive agent got fan mail from some broker promising the moon. They were wined and dined until they came to have an unrealistic idea of their worth. Knowing they were so sought-after gave them bravado, with no thought of how they got where they were. This resulted in the tail wagging the dog and there were those who no longer had a feeling of loyalty to their company.

It was interesting how some agents became impossible to work with once they were successful and others could take it gracefully in stride. I remember Jack Gibson, a fellow broker's *Statesman* ad, as he sought new agents for his company: "Heavy maintenance Barracudas and Prima Donnas need not apply." Amen to that!

Let the Party Begin

Socializing was a great way to build rapport between the agents, and parties helped all of us conquer stress, so at the drop of the hat, I would throw a party.

We had Christmas parties most every year at the beautiful Crystal Ballroom in the Hoff Building, complete with a banquet, bar and live music. Everyone came dressed to the teeth. There wasn't a wallflower among us as we all loved to dance. We often had Kevin Kirk and Sally Tibbs entertain us. They were great musicians and just right to dance to. We hung around as long as the musicians played.

We celebrated birthdays with lunches in our office, or out at a nearby restaurant. We always had a Christmas gift exchange where we drew names and every gift required a poem written to the giftee.

Another venue was The Stagecoach Restaurant and Bar. It had genuine funk in an old western way. It had never been updated although it had been there forever. The place had no windows and the lighting was iffy. The waitresses wore the same uniforms for as long as I can remember: skimpy black dresses that ended above the knee with white fringe around the bottom, on the sleeves and at the neck. I always thought they were a stab at looking like something an Indian maiden would wear. They were ghastly, but that was part of the funk. Before the smoking ordinance went into effect, the place was blue with cigarette smoke. But the food was delicious. They served tender steak and tasty seafood, the best in town. The place was a builders' hangout. The Talboy twins owned the Stagecoach, a business that was started by their father. Those girls were personable and charming and that may have had something to do with the restaurant's popularity.

Once, we entertained at the Stagecoach on a Sunday when it was generally closed and invited our builders and title-company friends. Everyone came in cowboy gear and we danced to bluegrass music until the wee hours.

42

When Boise's smoking ordinance took effect, it changed everything. The Stagecoach closed its doors in January of 2014.

We had ice cream socials in deference to our vintage building. Our garden came alive with balloons and parasols and the sounds of Gene Harris on piano. Jack loved jazz; he played a mean trumpet, so naturally he and Gene really hit it off. Gene became world famous before his untimely death. He was the best. We discovered him playing in the lobby of the Idan-ha Hotel in the 1980s. Jeano, Anne Stringer and I were so taken with him that I called Jack to hurry down and we sat for hours with a glass of wine enjoying Gene's music.

Phil Batt, once Idaho's governor, played his clarinet in a band we hired. The party gave us a chance to honor our clientele.

During the summer months, groups of us would retreat to McCall to stay at our cabin. Jack and I owned a big party boat so I would often take the gang around the lakefront in search of stylish cabins, or pack a lunch and go to a favorite cove.

Jack & Adelaide McLeod showing off their new logo.

The office crew: Kathi McLeod, Ann Erstad and Adelaide.

Tom and Adelaide going over the Tivoli Garden plans

Ice Cream Social. Front and center: Jenny Smith, Jean's daughter Jean with Adelaide and Tom McLeod on the left. Angie Tate and Anne Samuelsen to the right.

A broad view of the Garden Party.

Nina Cadwell and Jean Smith—If you've got it, flaunt it!

Jean-o strumming up some "country".

Anne Stringer, Pug Ostling and Jean Smith. Oh, yes, bankruptcy can be fun!

The Year of the Tiger

Ann Erstad looking chic. So that's what happened to all that toilet paper!

Kathy Jones in her "Maidenform" bonnet as Adelaide models her flower pot caddy.

Dianne Luce, Naomi Farber and Angie Tate at the hat party.

Pam Snow, Maggie Soderberg Simplot, Adelaide, Jean Smith, Ann Erstad, Naomi Farber and Anne Samuelsen at the cabin.

Relaxing on the party boat: Adelaide, Barbara Burnell, Dianne Luce, Kathy Jones and Naomi Farber.

Dianne Luce, Kathy Jones, Naomi Farber, Judy Wright, Ann Erstad and Angie Tate on the party boat.

The Incomparable Maggie Soderberg Simplot
in rare form.

Kathi McLeod twice as lovely as the wisteria she stands under.

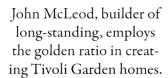

John McLeod, builder of long-standing, employs the golden ratio in creating Tivoli Garden homes.

Kevin McLeod, builder, does a masterful job of the one-level Craftsman homes in Tivoli Garden.

Left to right, bottom to top: Front Row: Margaret Burpee, Jean Smith, Rita Rodriguez, Anne Stringer, Adelaide McLeod. Second Row: Brit Peterson, Claudia Doege, Agnes Hoffman, Nina Cadwell, Todd Schaefer. Third Row: Gerry Soule, Carol Gill, Marsha Barney, T. J. Hill, Marilyn Hansen, Jeff Orr, Bob Mather. Fourth Row: Karen Berry, David Street, Pam Mosavassalani, Norma Cousins, Tom McLeod, Kathy Croner, Gail Holden.

A Jump into the Unknown

In the fall of 1985, my brother-in-law Griff phoned me from California and convinced me to buy a computer. They were new on the market; I knew nothing about them. But there was an excellent write-off for office machinery that year, so it piqued my interest. Those were the days that Jack made frequent trips to Portland to work on a computer as there were none in Boise. The one in Portland filled a thirty-foot-long room.

I bought a computer but once I had it, I didn't know what to do with it. Computers were so new to Idaho that there were no available classes to take; there were no handy computer gurus or any computer repair shops.

While I was struggling with this dilemma, a man drove up to the office in a yellow Fiat. He was trying to sell me on displaying our listings on a computer that he would situate in Albertson's grocery store. People who walked by could stop and view what we were marketing. Although I didn't pick up on his project, I was interested in him because he obviously knew something about computers. After explaining my problem to him, he said, "It would take some time going over your computer but, yes, I could help the clerical staff in learning to use it. It would cost you $700 for my services and I would have to have a key to the office." I was desperate, so I agreed. He showed up early every morning. When I walked in, he was always reading our newspaper and drinking our coffee. I don't remember ever seeing him in front of the computer. This went on for weeks and I finally questioned him. He gave me a rosy picture of his progress but said it was more involved than he thought it would be. I had given him $700 at the onset and was beginning to wonder about him.

One morning, he asked for a piece of carbon paper. Since the advent of our copying machine we no longer needed it and I combed the building and finally found a sheet of it in a desk.

Shortly thereafter, Jean Patrick came in to work on the books. She helped me one way or another since the inception of my company. First, she took telephone messages when I was an office of one. Later, she did my bookkeeping while our company was small, and she was kind enough to stick with it as we grew. She told everyone she wasn't a bookkeeper which translates: she had no training for it but she did a stellar job of it anyway.

She had a puzzled look on her face when she showed me that three checks were missing. They were way in the back of the book and it was amazing to me that she discovered they were gone. I called the bank and gave them the check numbers. Yes, two of them had been cashed and were signed by Kathi, who was the office receptionist. I put a stop-payment on the third and asked them to analyze Kathi's signature and sure enough, they called back in a few minutes, apologetic. The checks had been forged, there was no doubt about it. The bank would take responsibility for not catching that fact and we wouldn't lose any money.

Everything pointed to the computer guy. That's what he needed the carbon paper for. He hadn't made an appearance at the office since the day I gave it to him. The police were trying to find him.

Robert Jahn, a carpenter, was working on the sunroom. Robert often went to the library before he came to work and one day he spotted the familiar yellow Fiat just like the one the computer guy drove. So he looked around the library and sure enough there he was. Robert came to the office and told me. I called the police and they picked him up.

Kathi had to go to court to testify when they arraigned him because her name was on the checks. I went with her. When we walked past the computer guy in the courtroom he gave us a cheerful "good morning" as though nothing had happened. I was dumbfounded. He didn't have to serve time, nor was he penalized. If he had failed to put money in a parking meter, instead of forgery and theft, he would have been fined. It was his first offense; it would be on his record but that was it. I always wondered what kind of story he gave the court or if he was related to the judge.

Finally, Boise State University offered a computer class. Kathi, without my knowledge, took it upon herself to attend it, a good example of Kathi's commitment to her job. She had other attributes I admired: she didn't stoop to gossip and she was evenhanded when it came to working with agents.

Kathi diligently worked her way up the ladder, becoming office manager and finally broker a few years before we folded our tent.

Once, I had a listing in Sunset West. It was only an acre and it had a barn on it that could have served a hundred times that much ground. The subdivision was awkward because no one seemed to know what to do with an acre and parts of it went to weeds. The barn compounded the problem. I couldn't get anyone interested in buying the property until I realized I couldn't sell anything I didn't believe in, so I had to learn to love the barn. With that revelation, I touted the barn to buyers even before we reached the property. I told them how they could use it for a shop or a hobby room, keep a cow or chickens or even work on cars or what great storage it would make, and best of all, what fun it would be to have a barn dance and invite all their friends. Turning a disadvantage into an advantage, I sold the property.

One of the things I liked most about real estate was the people I met. It started with the agents I selected to join my company as I did a discriminating search to find those who had the right stuff. I liked to ask the person being interviewed if he or she ever participated in competitive sports. If the applicant didn't have that competitive gene in his makeup, it was certain he wasn't going to make it in real estate.

The most important part of putting a real estate transaction together is making sure it is a winning situation for all involved. I couldn't allow my buyer or seller to leave our office disgruntled. I was my business to make sure that never happened. That is why I did my own closings for years.

In the early eighties, I purchased a little machine called a Real-retrieve, a dandy little gadget. When hooked to a phone line it printed a Hot Sheet: the new listings that were not yet in the Multiple Listing book. In a way, it was a forerunner to the fax machine. I was working on it one morning when my friend and broker from United Realty, Bernie Moore, dropped by. He was aghast to find that I would spend money when business was down the toilet. Interest rates had climbed to 23% and Realtors were dropping out like flies. I had a plan and I wanted to share it with Bernie but I didn't because he was the competition.

There would be no doomsday talk coming from me. I knew that the positive environment in our office would encourage agents to see the bright side. The downturn was an opportunity to pick up business as there would be less competition. I knew we had to look prosperous, so I went right out and bought a new Mercedes. I called Jack to tell him the good news and he dropped by the dealership to take a look. He wasn't there five minutes, but when the title arrived in the mail, it was in Jack's name. As frustrating as that was, it didn't surprise me.

The dealer couldn't imagine putting the title to a car in a woman's name when she had a husband. In those days, even though my signature was on the checks I wrote as I paid the family bills and the mortgage on our home, I was considered a non-entity.

I popped into the First Security Bank trying to sort this situation out. How could I be in business and not exist? A high-ranking officer in the bank listened as I explained my dilemma. She told me, "You really ought to do something about that."

"I know. But what?" I asked.

"Well, you could take out a loan, even if you don't need one, and pay it off and that would establish your credit." I followed her advice and it worked.

Our company did an inordinate amount of business in Boise's North End. Of course, we covered the whole market as Boise was a small city. It was especially gratifying to take on refurbishing a North Ender because the neighbors down the block were inclined to follow suit. The North End had a special charisma because of its mature trees, its proximity to downtown and the many Craftsman houses that were worth updating and restoring.

During the sixties, before my time in real estate, many North Enders were hacked up and virtually destroyed by bad remodeling and modernizing. Many large homes became White Elephants and investors bought them to cut them up into apartments.

I have always been interested in architecture and especially in Boise's landmarks. I took it upon myself to do everything in my power to see that Boise's antiquity was preserved. While Jack and I were living in northern Montana where Jack was an engineer on the Hungry Horse Dam, we drove to Boise to see our parents. It was then that we discovered that our favorite landmark, the old City Hall, had been torn down. That made me more aware of just how important preservation is. Once a building is gone, it's gone, and there is no getting it back.

Barzie Young and some of his friends were rallying to save the Eastman Building at Eighth and Main streets. I contributed a real-estate commission to help fund their effort. They were so pleased that they gave me a lovely etching of the Eastman Building. It was a sure thing; the building would be saved. Sadly, before the actual work began, some homeless folks started a fire in the building to keep warm. The building burned and what was left was carted away.

A fellow broker, who I dare not name, had the habit of trying to put me down. It seemed to be a game with him. He made it clear that women didn't belong in the man's world of real estate. The last time he heckled me, I retorted with, "You chauvinist, cut it out. I've read *The Art of Intimidation*, too." That put an end to it and in the years to come, we became friends, but, of course, on my terms.

On the Seedy Side

In the early eighties, a United States Marshall came to the office. Behind closed doors he told me: "I need your help. Could you find a house for some people who are on the Witness Protection Program? Your attorney, Lou Cosho, said that you could be trusted. Secrecy is paramount. You don't need to worry about the money; it will be forthcoming. Would you help them find a home?"

"Sure, I will," I said.

I made an appointment with the people the next morning and as I drove out the old Mountain Home highway to a sleazy motel, I began to wonder what I had gotten myself into. I rapped on the door and saw the window curtain move. Finally, the door opened a crack to reveal an ill-groomed, emaciated woman. After I stepped inside, my eyes slowly adjusted to the poorly lit room. There stood a grisly hunk of man, naked to the waist, whose hairy flab was hanging over his pants. He was the one being protected? I mused. My first impulse was to get out of there . . . fast! But I couldn't. I had a job to do.

As I drove these strange people from subdivision to subdivision showing them houses, I learned they had two children who would come as soon as their parents were settled. They would be given new names, new identities, even their school records would be fictitious. The man had been in the restaurant business but he would have to find a different line of work. I was relieved when we found a house the first day out and I could be done with it. A $10,000 earnest money check arrived by courier. My job was almost finished. The closing would occur in a couple of weeks.

A few days later, the U. S. Marshall stood over my desk again. The man, my buyer, a habitual gambler, had been spotted at the racetrack by the Mafia. Yes, the <u>Mafia</u>, that's what he said. The Marshall would have to relocate them once again. In the middle of the night, they boarded a government plane and were spirited off to parts unknown. The earnest money? Split it with the seller, just the way the agreement reads. Although that was customarily how it was done, I was hesitant to keep the money if the transaction didn't come to fruition. It just didn't seem fair. But it was different because that's what the Marshall wanted me to do and he wouldn't have it any other way. So after I gave the seller his half of the money, the Salvation Army got a sizable boost from me that Christmas.

Agnes Hoffman came into my office with her earnest money agreement in hand. "I have been working with a Russian Orthodox couple who wanted to buy a church," she said. "There was one on the market for $70,000 and I took them to see it. It met their needs and they asked me to write a full-price offer which they signed and I went to look for the seller. After the seller read it, he countered it at $60,000. I don't get it. Why would a seller do that?" Agnes asked.

I read the agreement and the counter as well. "Yes, that does seem odd but there is nothing illegal about it," I said. "If the seller wants to sell for $60,000 instead of $70,000, it is your buyer's good fortune."

The buyers, who were Russian Orthodox clergy, must have thought it was a gift from God.

The highlight of one beautiful summer day was bizarre and at the same time laughable. Herb Shiremire, one of my agents, had a customer who was looking for property in Warm Springs Mesa. The subdivision had been a hard sell due to the publicity it had received because of some unstable ground where the home-sites stood far above the highway below. Unfortunately, there was a landslide which made some people believe that the whole development was unstable, which it wasn't. Because of the bad press, market values plummeted and a few people who did their homework thought it was a great investment.

Warm Springs Mesa, east of downtown Boise on Highway 21, was in the foothills backing up to Tablerock. Close in, it was a desirable place to live except for the concern about the landside. Herb checked the Multiple Listing Service and made a trek through the winding, hilly streets looking for an available property. Finding nothing, he resorted to knocking on doors.

Paul Wise, the developer of the Mesa, opened his door to Herb. When Herb asked him if he wanted to sell, Paul was quick to say he would. Herb wrote up an earnest money agreement after his customers toured the house. Herb turned the paperwork over to me and I spent the usual time analyzing it. Satisfied, I put it in the pending file.

The next morning, Paul Wise showed up at my office door. He wanted to see the earnest money agreement.

"Didn't you get a copy?" I asked.

"Well, yes. But I'd like to see the original." That was an odd request, but I asked the secretary to bring it in. Paul seemed very anxious as I placed it in front of him. After looking it over, he closed the file folder and placed it on his lap. Then the folder found its way behind his back as he chatted away about how nice my office was. Five minutes transpired as he made a stab at small talk.

Then, suddenly, he jumped to his feet, and with a crazed look on his face, he bolted out the front door taking the file with him. I was stunned. It was clear what had happened. Paul had second thoughts about selling. Perhaps his wife wasn't in agreement. We'll never really know.

Herb was upset. No one likes to lose a sale. "What can we do about it?" he wanted to know.

"Really nothing," I told him. "Given the facts, there is no way to make Mr. Wise sell if he has changed his mind and doesn't want to. We could seek damages but how damaged is anyone when the transaction only came together yesterday? Your best bet is to look for another property," I said with conviction. Life goes on as the stomach churns. Herb eventually found another house for his customer.

When I walked into the office one Monday morning, things were in an uproar. Marilyn Hansen, the cat lover of all time, seemed be the center of it. Everyone was laughing.

"What's going on? I want in on the joke," I told them.

"Well," Marilyn said, with a smirk on her face, "my cat crawled into the dryer this morning."

"And you turned the dryer on?" I asked.

"Well, not exactly. I just closed the door and dryer started to run. There was a lot of thumping and yowling. And I finally realized my kitty was in there, so I opened the door."

"Oh, my goodness, that's horrible. How is the kitty?" I asked.

"Fluffy," she answered.

It is funny about cats. Almost everyone who has been in real estate for any length of time hates cats, except for Marilyn Hansen, of course. It is unbelievable how many homes reek of cat odor. There have been occasions when I had to leave a house we were touring because of the ghastly cat smell. It makes my eyes tear and my stomach churn. It is hard to understand how people can live with that, but they do.

Imagine how difficult it was when we were caught trying to market a "cat house." My advice to potential sellers is to get rid of the indoor litter box, put the cat outside on the hour, and buy a case of Febreze. If your cat is senile and forgets himself, rip up the carpet, scrub the floor with Lysol and have a new carpet installed.

I was especially fond of a young couple in our office: Susie and Jeff Orr. Susie was receptionist and Jeff was a Realtor. They were about to have their second child. When it was close to her time, I hired a "temp" to take over until Susie could come back.

Jean Smith, Anne Stringer and I were having a bite to eat at Anne's as we talked about our concerns for the Orrs. They were having trouble and they obviously needed a little help. It wasn't like them to squabble but they seemed to be doing that most of the time.

"Maybe we should let Jeff's parents know. They seemed really nice when they came up to visit," Jean said.

"Why don't we call them and tell them what's going on," I said. All we knew was that Jeff's Dad was a doctor who lived in La Jolla, California.

Anne picked up the phone and asked for information. "I'm looking for Dr. Robert Orr's telephone number in La Jolla, California," she told the operator. She wrote the number down and dialed it. A man answered. "Are you Dr. Robert Orr?" Anne asked.

"Yes. How can I help you?"

"This is Anne Stringer. Susie and Jeff are having some problems getting along; it's just not like them. We thought maybe you could come to Boise and help them out. You know their baby is due anytime now. Jean, Adelaide and I don't know how to help them and we thought you could find a way to get them back on track. They're great kids but they're under a lot of stress just now. Can you come?"

"I don't know who you're talking about. You must have the wrong Dr. Orr," he said.

There was a long silence before Anne said, "Does that mean you aren't coming?"

Just in from a tour, Jeff got a phone call. It was Susie telling Jeff he had better come quick. Jeff mumbled, "What in heck am I going to do with Josh when I take Susie to the hospital?"

"I'll take care of Josh," I said. It had been a long time since my kids were two so I was a little rusty when it came to taking care of little ones, but someone had to help. I hopped in my car and drove out to their house. Jeff was frantically trying to get Susie in the car while Josh was in the house in the bathtub playing with his toys. I wrapped Josh up in a big towel and carried him out to the car just as Jeff was starting up the engine. Josh and I waved "good-bye" and went back into the house. I dried and powdered Josh and set him in his crib while I looked for clothes. The window was open and there was a warm, gentle breeze sifting into the room. The phone rang and I went out to the kitchen to answer it and just then the breeze blew the bedroom door shut.

Normally, that wouldn't be any problem but Jeff had taken the doorknob off to keep Josh confined to his bedroom. I looked all over for the doorknob but couldn't find it.

I called my son John and asked if he could help me out. Yes, he'd be right there. Josh was crying and I was unable to comfort him through the door, so I went outside and around to the open bedroom window. I took off my high heels and climbed up on a wood pile outside Josh's room. As I climbed into the bedroom my feet were dangling and the Orrs' little dog growled and nipped at my toes. What a good little watchdog!

When I finally managed to climb through the window, I held Josh and he quit crying. I dressed him and was wondering what I should do next when John showed up and freed us from the bedroom. I put Josh in my car and headed for the office.

As I was telling the gang all about it, I realized that in all the excitement, I hadn't put Josh in a diaper. I ran home to change my clothes.

While Josh was still very little he greeted everyone in the office by name. He was very smart. Now he is grown and married and has a little boy of his own.

One of the agents in my office left this plaque on my desk:

"I MUST HURRY AS I AM THEIR LEADER AND THERE THEY GO!"

There was some truth in it. My agents were so energetic, I sometimes had to pump hard just to keep up. This great group of Type "A" personalities put a smile on the face of real estate. They were strong, independent women.

Their common denominator was real estate, yet beyond that I discovered close friendships budding between them, some of which have lasted a lifetime. It's hard to imagine all that energy under one roof; it was extraordinary and I felt proud to be a part of it.

Ann Samuelsen, Maggie Soderberg, June Gerhardt, Carole Gill and Nancy Goble rode together in the same car when we went on tour. They became good friends and started a tradition of celebrating birthdays together, and they still do. Nancy moved to San Francisco, so they all hopped a plane and went down to celebrate Nancy's birthday. Jean Smith regularly sees Nina Cadwell, Anne Stringer -- who lives in Southern California -- Rita Rodrigez and me. Naomi Farber, Dianne Luce and Judy Arnt became pals and hiked together to many interesting places. Agnes Hoffman and Brit Peterson had an ongoing friendship. I see most of them from time to time for lunch or when we can find any old excuse to throw a party. There was something extraordinary about the dynamics in our office that is beyond explaining – you had to be there.

We had very few squabbles. The only one that comes to mind was the "perfume war." One agent used quite a lot of perfume. At a desk close by, another agent had terrible perfume allergies. The situation became ugly and they called on me to settle it. "It's really up to you two to work it out," I said. One of them moved to another room and that ended it. It would be nice if all disputes were so easily rectified.

Becky Stinson and her husband Stan were a heck of a team. Stan built the houses and Becky sold them. They got an offer on a Lakewood home from a couple moving to Boise from out of state. The house was finished and ready for the buyers to move in. On closing day, the buyer's Realtor called about a half hour before the buyer was to sign, telling Becky the buyer was not going to close the deal. He was having second thoughts about spending that much money and he prayed to God about it. God told him not to buy the house. Becky was furious and called her attorney. He drafted a letter, and hand-carried it to the buyer informing him that to the best of his knowledge, God did not have a broker's license and as Stinsons' attorney he advised the buyer to close. And he did.

One Friday evening in late January, Jack went to the office to take some measurements to facilitate taking in the back porch. He had forgotten his key and looked for a way to get in. He found the first-floor bathroom window unlocked and he climbed in and got busy with his measuring tape when a booming voice accosted him: "Come out with your hands up." Jack went to the window to discover the building was surrounded by the police with their weapons drawn. Jack was shaken up. He gathered his nerve and went out to talk to them with his hands over his head, of course. Somehow, he was able to convince the police that he was the owner of the building. The woman across the street had seen Jack from her kitchen window as he crawled into our building and thought she was witnessing a break-in. Jack called it a day and came home.

Our office was broken into and robbed twice. The first time we figured it was kids who had entered through a window. They took the stamps, the petty cash and pried the pop machine open for the quarters. But the second time was much worse. The burglars were professional. They used a crowbar on the front door to get in. They stole our grandfather clock, wrapping it in an oriental carpet. They took new computers and left the older ones behind. They took a printer and an expensive camera, leaving the crowbar on the floor and walking out the back door. I was grateful they hadn't spotted the bronze sculpture.

The police told us the crooks left the crowbar so they couldn't be caught with it and they advised me to install locks that secured the doors from the inside, so you had to have a key to leave the building.

In time, the police recovered my computer and returned it to me. John and Tom were checking it out and discovered that the thieves had used my camera and taken pictures of themselves using a bong. There was also a photo of a girl whose eyes were all pupil.

I didn't get the camera or the printer back or for that matter, any of the other loot.

About a month later, Jack and I were just arriving home from McCall to find the phone ringing. Nina Cadwell was on the other end. "Could you come down to the office and let me out?" she asked.

When we pulled up to the building, there was Nina, like a caged animal, with both hands on the window looking out. It was almost comical. She told us she had been trying to find a way to get out of the building for two hours. She had run into the building leaving her keys in her car and while she was there whoever was in the building left and locked the door. Fortunately, Nina took it in stride but I was more than a little appalled that I had created such a booby trap.

It was Tuesday morning again and the agents were touting their new listings. An agent went on and on and on about her listing. The owners were very important people and the seller might be home when we toured it. Then, in a condescending tone, she admonished us all to be on our best behavior. I couldn't believe my ears. It was so demeaning.

It was as though she were the Mother Superior and we were the naughty children. Eyebrows raised as the agents looked from one to the other. If there had been any way to ignore that house on tour, I'm sure they would have. However, we did tour the house and thank goodness, the owner wasn't home because Todd Shaefer came a little late and made his grand entrance. There was a long piece of toilet paper hanging out the back of his pants. Todd was such a cutup. It was like him to come up with something like that. The tension evaporated as we all broke into uncontrollable laughter.

It was Sunday morning and time for "The Real Estate Connection" hosted by McLeod Realty. Jean Smith and Nina Cadwell were the stars on KIDO radio, at nine o'clock Sunday mornings. It was a call-in show and they tried to have an "expert" on with them to interview, such as an attorney, a lender or an appraiser. There weren't many call-ins and when there were, they were usually from some small town like Weiser, Melba or Middleton – places Jean and Nina had never been – and not from the Boise area, so there was little chance of a call-in becoming a customer. In fact, there weren't many people listening to the radio on Sunday morning. So they had to get people to call in – like Jack McLeod, Nina's son Dave, or Jean's daughter Jenny's high school pals.

Their specialty – when no one called in and they ran out of topics – was describing the subtle differences between town-homes, patio homes and condominiums. They could go on forever on that topic.

They had a theme song: "Buy Real Estate While You Can" –sung by Jean with her guitar.

You better buy it while you can.
You better buy it while you can.
If you wait too long, it will all be gone
And you'll be sorry then . . .
It doesn't matter if you're rich or not
It's the same for a woman or a man,
From the cradle to the crypt
Is a mighty short trip
Buy real estate while you can.

We came to the conclusion that there weren't many people listening to the radio and sadly, "The Real Estate Connection" faded away.

One year, on February 15, Jack and I were coming back from a South America vacation and missed our international flight. It was disastrous because I was the speaker for the annual Chamber of Commerce breakfast on February 17, and I wanted a day to get over my jetlag and organize my thoughts. I was still in a euphoria after visiting the ethereal Iguaçu Falls and Machu Picchu and I couldn't seem to come down off my cloud. We arrived in Boise late in the day of February 16, which left me no time to hone my speech or figure out what I was going to wear.

It was a big affair: hundreds of people attended. It was important to me because I was one of the first female speakers at the Chamber of Commerce breakfast, which was still dominated by men. I had to do a good job because I felt like I was representing all women in business and, of course, there was the matter of our company's reputation. I was a little nervous as I looked out over the sea of faces and then I saw many of them were smiling at me, as though they were anticipating my every word. That was all it took.

I was well-versed in residential real estate so I was in my element. I amazed myself as I took control of the receptive audience, and felt like I had cut the mustard as I was well received. But as soon as it was over, I went home and crawled into bed and slept twelve hours.

I once listed a little home that belonged to an elderly widow, Virgie Cline. While I was marketing it, we became good friends. She told me that when the house sold, she and her friend, Mary Beth, were going to move to California where the winters were mild. She was having her 1960 Cadillac repaired so they could make the trip.

I figured Mary Beth must be a younger woman if they were going to drive all that distance, but when I met her I discovered she was older than Virgie and she didn't know how to drive.

"Virgie, why don't you just fly down?" I asked. "It would be easier. California is a long way away."

"Oh, I can't do that, Virgie said. "I've had my Caddy for years – it's like a member of the family. My husband gave it to me for my birthday the year before he died."

The house sold and after it was closed, I popped by to see Virgie. She was busy packing her things. "What would you do if you have car trouble down on the desert?" I asked. I tried one more time to talk her out of driving, but I was whistling in the wind.

My only option was to rig up a "care basket" with a first-aid kit, a flashlight and an assortment of snacks. Then I asked her to call me as soon as she got to Riverside or sooner if she was having trouble. She agreed.

It was at least three days before she called. "Well, we made it to Riverside in one piece, but you were right -- flying down would have been easier. Why didn't I listen to you?"

"What went wrong?" I asked.

"Well, let's see, just about everything. Mary Beth got nauseated and threw up in the car and it has smelled yucky ever since. We're not getting along too well. I cleaned it up but I couldn't get rid of the smell. If she'd only told me she was going to be sick, I could have stopped the car. I let her lie down in the back seat until she felt better. Then, the car stopped running out on the desert and I couldn't get it going again, so I tried to flag down passing cars, but no one would stop. Finally, a truck driver towed us into Reno where a mechanic put in a new fuel pump; that was expensive. We stayed overnight in a horrible motel. The beds were the worst and the lady behind the counter, who checked us in, looked like a prostitute. Do you think we were in a bordello?"

"Oh, I hardly think so, but it's a good thing you are out of there," I said.

"We had a little lunch in Bishop and when I drove back onto the highway, I got confused and headed the wrong way and we ended up back in Reno so we spent another night there," she said.

"Really. How awful. I hope you didn't go back to the same motel," I said.

"No, we didn't but this one was worse. The bathroom was a mile down the hall which was a problem for me because I get up several times during the night.

"Once we got going the next morning, a sheriff stopped me on the highway. He said I was going too slow. Can you imagine that? Well, anyway, he didn't give me a ticket.

"I picked up a kid who was hitchhiking and let him drive the car but not for long, because he drove too darn fast. He smoked cigarettes, one after another, and I was afraid Mary Beth would get sick again, so I made him stop. But the smoke seemed to cover up the smell of the vomit for a little while.

Anyway, he is a nice kid; his name is Bennie and he helped me find my cousin April's house once we reached Riverside." I thought, Virgie, you're lucky to be alive.

"I let him drive again because all that traffic going into Riverside gave me the heebie-jeebies," Virgie said. "Other than that, everything is fine. April rented a nice little house for us. The movers arrived before we did and piled the stuff everywhere. Thank goodness, April told them to put the beds in the bedrooms; they're too big for me to move.

Bennie says he is going to stick around until we get settled so he can help us. Isn't that nice of him? He'll have to sleep on the couch. We're in walking distance from April's house. It's only three blocks away."

"Thanks again for the snacks -- they really kept us going. Bennie liked the cookies. Oh, yes, I think I'm going to sell my car." I breathed a sigh of relief at that good news.

A Developing Story

As time went by, our company marketed a few subdivisions and I dabbled a little in development. The most noteworthy were Warm Springs Woods, in east Boise; Shady Beach in McCall on the upper prong of Payette Lake and Tivoli Garden at Lake Harbor in west Boise. The risk is high in developing, but sometimes, so is the profit.

In 1981, my involvement in Warm Springs Woods came about when son Tom was keeping his horse in a pasture off Lewis Street just south of Warm Springs Avenue. It was separated by an old railroad track from Municipal Park, and just blocks from our East Hays Way home. I became interested in the land and managed to buy a few acres and that's where I met my friend Ernie Lombard, a local architect who was doing the same thing. Somehow, Larry Leisure got involved. After finding the three-way partnership too cumbersome, Ernie and I decided the best thing for us to do was sell the property.

We offered the property to Marv Simpson, a local builder. He had immediate interest and started an attached housing complex: triplexes and duplexes. There hadn't been much attached housing in Boise and buyers, at that time, were leery of something so new. The market was flat and the sales were happening at a snail's pace.

I thought that if I furnished a unit vignette-style, a buyer might find it more appealing. With an easy chair, a footstool, end table, a copy of the Wall Street Journal and a pair of glasses, I tried to give the living room more interest. But business was lagging and my effort didn't seem to be enough. Sales were still very slow and Marv wanted me to buy the development back.

I had made two sales before this happened: I sold a unit in the triplex to my friend Ann Wyatt who recently had been widowed and wanted to move out of her big home. In the process of moving, she found a number of gold bricks wrapped like meat in the bottom of her freezer in the basement. Then, going through her late husband's desk, she found a deed to a property on a Central American island that she had never heard about. She became more cautious about what she threw away and a little angry as well when she realized her husband had kept secrets from her. She couldn't help but wonder if there was anything else she hadn't discovered.

She bought the west end of the triplex that we called the "tree house" because a huge maple tree sat on the back of its lot.

The other sale I made was to our close friends, Pat and Jean Patrick. I didn't like the idea of leaving them hanging without neighbors and only bare ground surrounding them. I couldn't stand the idea they might regret the fact that they had moved into the project at its infancy. I felt I needed to rectify the situation and both Jack and I could see good potential with a shift in concepts. We settled with Marv and re-subdivided Warm Springs Woods into single-dwelling lots. The market in Boise was still slow but by offering lots to builders I knew, it eventually built out. Now, years later, Warm Springs Woods has become one of the most desirable subdivisions in the East End.

Don Gile and Bill Deasy owned land to the east, separated from Warm Springs Woods by just a block or so of junky houses, they called Warm Springs Woods East. They wanted to develop it and asked me to do the marketing. My first assignment was acquisition of the dilapidated houses so they could be torn down, which would enhance their project and give them more land. So I started my door-knocking campaign.

First, I met an old lady who had lived in the house her whole life. "The only way I'll leave is feet first," she said. "I don't have the energy to move."

"If you change your mind, please give me a call," I said as I handed her my business card.

Next, came an East Junior High teacher who lived underground as somehow construction came to a halt after the basement was built. He liked his "digs" just fine.

Late in the day, I knocked on a door to have a young man answer it buck naked. I was appalled. "I want to talk to you -- how about getting some clothes on?" I growled.

"I could do that," he said as he disappeared. Come to find out he was only a renter. The property belonged to his grandmother who lived in Cascade.

I approached the last house and asked the owner if he was interested in selling. He jumped at the chance because he was afraid the new developments that surrounded him were bound to raise his taxes.

I asked him if he would like me to help him find a new home and he was eager. His work had been in mining but now he was retired. There were fingers missing from both of his hands. I couldn't tell if he was born that way or if he'd had an accident. He told me he would like to live in a smaller community where taxes were lower and housing was cheaper. We decided on Emmett, about thirty miles from Boise. His wife rolled up the street on her three-wheel bike. She had just finished touring the East End alleys looking for salvage. I got the feeling she was impaired.

I was a little anxious about how I would deal with them and asked Jack if he would go along. The two of us piled in the Mercedes and drove to their house. Jack, always the gentleman, hopped out of the car to greet them.

The woman slid past Jack and into the front passenger seat. The man and his son and his son's friend popped into the back. Jack was left standing there wondering what in heck he should do. Very nicely, he said, "I think I'll walk over to Pat's and see what he's doing." What a guy!

Once we arrived in Emmett, we marched into a local diner for a little lunch. The waitress seemed very much amused by my entourage and as much as I hate to admit it, I felt a little embarrassed.

The first house I showed them seemed to fit the bill. It seemed almost too easy. Yet, it was offered at such a low price, there would be a big residual when they closed on their Boise home. I liked that. It would be nice to put money in his pocket because it was obvious he needed it. He wanted to stop by the bank to open an account. When I pulled in the parking lot, he asked me if I would go in with him, so I did. Evidently, he felt unsure of himself. On the way home, he made jabs at me, saying I was trying to get his family out of the neighborhood. By the time I stopped at their house, I was really undone. Had I said something to make him feel that way? Was he having seller's remorse? Almost every day for the next couple of weeks he would call me at the office with questions about his move and often asked me to come by to talk to him.

The title company called and wanted to close early on the transaction, in fact that afternoon. Was it possible? "I'll call the seller and see what I can do. The sellers won't be moving until the first of the month. Do you know that?"

"No. I'm glad you told me. Will they pay rent?"

"No, no rent."

I called the seller and he agreed to the early closing. When I went to pick them up, I could tell the man had brushed his hair and made a stab at cleaning up, but his wife jumped in my car wearing a dress that was covered with many days of food stains and a pair of dirty flip flops. Once again, I was a little embarrassed when the three of us marched into the title company.

After closing, the man called and asked me to come by his house. I had a horrible feeling he wanted out of the deal and at this point there was nothing I could do about it.

I knocked on his door and when he opened it, he handed me a beautiful little clock he had made out of a walnut tree he had harvested out of his back yard. I was so touched, I wanted to cry. This man without the use of good hands had made this clock for me. What a lesson in humility that was.

I had to be careful what I chose to do outside the office as I had limited free time. I sat on several boards including the original board for the Idaho Botanical Garden during its infancy. Christopher Davidson, with a PhD in Botany, worked incessantly to get it going. I was so impressed with what he had accomplished, I wanted to help.

"Would you have time in your busy life to establish an iris garden?" he asked.

"I'd sure like to try," I said.

I asked Liz Blaine if she would help me. Through the years, she and I shared our love of gardening with an emphasis on tall bearded irises. "I'd love to do that," she said.

We decided that if we were going to do the right thing for the Botanical Garden, each plant needed to be identified with a metal marker with its name and the date it was introduced. We couldn't create a proper iris garden without including all of the Dyke's Medal Winners: the iris voted the best new introduction of the year since 1932 when it was all started by the American Iris Society. Some of the oldest Dykes were hard to come by. It was a tedious endeavor, but in time and by contacting iris growers in Boise and throughout the country, we amassed the complete collection. It was more work than either of us thought it would be.

Before the iris garden was complete, Christopher went on to greater things. He is searching for undiscovered flora all over the world to photograph and identify for posterity. One day, he will have amassed a complete encyclopedia of the world's plants.

The Dyke's Medal Winners were lined along a path in chronological order and well-marked so that they would reveal a meaningful history of irises in America. This completed, we decided we needed a map to list the irises and where we planted them in case some of our markers disappeared. We included a photo of each variety. I took every minute I could scrape up to create the map. I'm the first to admit that growing irises is continuous work. They are hearty and will grow anywhere but they won't bloom unless the clumps are divided every three years and the rhizomes that have the blooming stem are discarded. I had given all the time I could afford to the Botanical Garden and I am sad to say, the Iris Garden was never properly cared for and is basically gone. Sometimes, despite the best of intentions, our work comes to naught. But that doesn't mean we should quit trying.

****

Jack and I both loved McCall and it became our getaway when we could manage it. We had purchased a cabin on leased ground in Pilgrim Cove from the Frisbees. Patty Frisbee knew all the gossip on that part of the lake and told me one day that Clem Parberry was retiring from coaching at the University of Idaho and would likely be selling Shady Beach Cabin Camp, next door to Pilgrim Cove. Clem and his wife Viola ran the cabin camp in summers, and Clem coached for the University of Idaho winters.

The camp had been there as long as I could remember. Almost everyone I knew had stayed there sometime or another, including our family. It was a gorgeous property, nicely wooded with 800 feet of lakefront with a sandy beach and a view down the narrows: the Girl Scout camp to the left and Luck's Point to the right, all the way to North Beach. Spectacular! What a grand subdivision it would make. I called Clem Parberry and got an appointment with him on a Thursday to see if the rumor was true. "Yes, I'm going to sell Shady Beach," he said.

"Well, I am very interested in the property and would like to buy it from you," I said.

We toured the property and he told me all the things he thought I should know including what he thought the property was worth; I felt he was reasonable.

We had a deal! We made a date to meet the next weekend to iron out the details. We shook hands on it. Sunday, three days later, Clem had a heart attack and dropped dead on the dock.

I'm no ambulance chaser so I didn't bother the family by harassing them to make good on Clem's deal with me. I felt they would honor my offer when the time was right.

As we drove home from McCall, the canyon road with all its twists and turns, its beautiful forest delighted me and then I fell into a slump as the evergreens disappeared, and the bare hills seemed desolate and disturbing. "Back to reality," I said with a sigh.

"Do you want me to turn the car around and go back to the cabin?" Jack asked as he gave my knee a love pat.

"I can't. I've already been away from the office too long."

"You know, Dreamboat," Jack said, "as much as we love McCall, I don't think either of us are meant to be there full time. That would be too much of a good thing. You know, like all icing, and no cake."

"You're right. It wouldn't be so delicious."

One day, Marv Simpson brought a developer, Jon Barnes, into my office. Marv had told Jon that I was a problem solver. I wondered where he got that idea. Marv reminded me how I had bailed him out of Warm Springs Woods. Jon was having problems with his subdivision, Greyloch. It seemed that the covenants required side-loaded garages, and Marv was building the first house in the subdivision and had almost finished it before he realized that the lot was too narrow to accommodate the driveway needed to get into the garage.

"Have you any ideas about how we can solve the problem?" Jon asked.

"How many lots are sold?" I asked.

"Only three. The word got out that the lots were too narrow for side-loaded garages," Jon said.

"Give me the names of the builders who have closed on their lots and I'll see what I can do. It might be a good idea to go out to your project to get a better perspective," I said.

After looking at Marv's house, it was obvious that the only way to solve the problem was to increase the size of the lot. That meant that the lot next-door would lose some width. Fortunately, there would be enough width left on the next door lot if the garage was front-loaded.

"That won't work," Jon said. "We can't have front-loaded garages. It says so in the covenants."

"We'll have to change the covenants," I said.

"It's too late for that," Jon said. "The covenants have been recorded."

"You need to talk to your attorney. I feel pretty sure you can change the covenants if all the owners agree to it. The changes will also be recorded. This is messy business and will take some money for the attorney and a re-survey, but I think it's the best way out," I said.

It was a tedious process, but we got it straightened out. After that, Jon cracked me up when he dubbed me: *The First Lady of Real Estate*. Then, he hired Tom to market Greyloch Subdivision.

One of the nicest experiences I had in my real-estate career was marketing Nature's Wood Duck Island and getting to know Sandi Johnson, the on-site partner of the development consortium. It was inspiring to watch Sandi take a piece of land along the Boise River and develop it with such sensitivity that twenty-seven acres were set aside as common area, mostly waterways and wetlands, and thirteen acres in a wildlife preserve where the heron rookery became legendary.

The ground being subdivided was once farmland and some environmentalists felt that the wildlife would be displaced, but quite the contrary occurred. As the landscaping of homes progressed it created a safe haven for ducks, geese, numerous other birds, otters, squirrels, and beavers, and there was far more wildlife than there had been before. It was a classy development with a number of Boise's best builders and our marketing team.

We established a tight schedule for marketing: every step of our advertising and promotion was planned. Our Grand Opening was imminent.

The bridge at the entrance of the development crossed the canal. Somehow, the engineer made a mistake in measuring the bridge's height and it had to be torn out and replaced. That changed everything. I couldn't start on an advertising campaign and then stop. The reputation of the development was at stake. It was our job to keep interest piqued during the many months while the entrance bridge was being rebuilt. Our "Coming Soon!" wore thin and we were spending advertisement dollars in the Idaho Statesman that we would never recover, but that's how it sometimes goes. In spite of the long delay the marketing was still profitable for us and the development was a huge success.

Back to McCall. Our family went to the cabin for the Fourth of July. The fireworks on the lake were always spectacular and we needed a break. Two years had slipped by since Clem Parberry's sudden death. While Tom and I were out sailing on his catamaran, a heavy rainstorm took us off the lake to sit around the fireplace and read a good book. My book was boring and I became restless. I jumped into my car, without any destination in mind, and drove over to Shady Beach Cabin Camp. As I reached the lodge, Larry Parberry, Clem's son, was hanging onto the screen door.

"Hey, Larry, have you folks had any thoughts of selling?" I asked. "I'm still interested."

He yelled back through the drizzle. "It's strange you'd come today. If it hadn't been for the rain, we would all be out on the lake instead of being holed-up in the lodge. We came to a decision. It's time to sell."

I was so excited. The Parberrys would keep 200 feet of lakeshore frontage and build a family cabin there and would leave 600 feet of lakefront.

There hadn't been a lakefront sale like this for as long as I could remember. There had been lakefront condo complexes: Brown's Palace, Tamarack Bay, Elevation Five Thousand, Crystal Beach and Water's Edge; but none had a piece of ground like this.

If the word got out there would be a dozen developers vying for it. It was a miracle. Time surely was of the essence. I wondered just what it was that spirited me to Shady Beach that particular day. On our trip back to Boise, I took out my yellow pad and worked on the time line for the development. It would take more than one summer because of the short building season.

Developing on Payette Lake wasn't going to be easy and I knew it. Folks who had cabins around the lake were desperately trying to protect the beautiful but fragile lake. I couldn't blame them as I felt the same way.

Payette Lake was magic for those of us who were lucky enough to be there. The lake people had adopted a no-growth mindset. The Planning and Zoning commissioners in Valley County and the City of McCall echoed their no-growth mantra. There would be a lot of flack over what I wanted to do. Somehow, I had to win the summer folks over.

Once I found out who the no-growth people were, I asked for an audience with them. They were willing and I took Lou Cosho, my friend and attorney with me. I needed someone on my side. I told my story and once the group realized I was actually going to decrease the density from forty-five cabins that were occupied 24/7 all summer long to a development of twenty cottages, their fears subsided and I got their blessing.

A Hiatis

After we got home, my sister Jane, who owned a travel agency -- Griffin Travel -- called me in the middle of the night and asked if I would go to Israel with her.

"How exciting. When are you going?"

"That's just it. Next Saturday. I have travelers depending on me and the girl who was going to be my roommate and helper flaked."

"I'll have to see if someone can take over for me. How long would we be gone?" I asked.

"Two weeks. I know this isn't very much notice but I really need you. I'm taking thirty-two Catholics to the Holy Land. We are scheduled to go to Vienna and then Rome for a few days before we come home."

"It sounds too good to be true. I'll see if I can find someone to take the brokerage over while I'm gone and call you back in the morning," I said.

Jack woke up and asked, "Who are you talking to?"

"It's Jane and she wants me to go to Israel with her. What do you think?"

His head was on his pillow as he closed his eyes. "Tomorrow. Can't we talk about it over coffee?"

"Of course, we can." But I was so excited, I couldn't go back to sleep. Everything worked out and I met Jane in San Francisco where, on Saturday, we boarded an international flight.

It was the experience of a lifetime, like stepping into a time machine that took us back 2,000 years. Things you expected to be gone were miraculously still there. Jerusalem's narrow cobblestone street – The Via Dolorosa, the Way of Sorrow, where Jesus carried the cross – appeared much like it must have so long ago. Small open shops lined the street where you might find candles, prayer carpets, blown-glass and falafels.

On the desert below, Bedouins were herding sheep and goats from one oasis to another. The mosques, churches and synagogues were intermingled. I couldn't help but wonder, when there are so many similarities between their beliefs, if they originally came from the same genesis. Mohammad ascended to become immortal, just as Jesus did. So many people have interpreted what was written through the years and so many factions have splintered off the original intention, that it seems possible. The Bible, the Qur'an, and the Tanakh Tora, have many differences but also bear many similarities. It isn't too far fetched to think that in the beginning, the three religions. may have had the same origin.

A Change in Plans

The day after I got home I met two young Iranian men who had just graduated from the University of Idaho. Our mutual friend, Rick Vycital brought them into my office.

They were looking for a lakefront in McCall. I found a dandy for them, an old log cabin that was especially charming and a lakefront. It belonged to an attorney who had inherited it from his family. It filled the bill so the Iranians signed an agreement at the seller's listed price.

I took the agreement to the seller and he was impressed by the clean sale but decided he wanted to exclude the wood pile so he countered the offer. I was quick to remind the attorney that with a counter, the buyers had the right to refuse the counter and be out of the deal. He let the counter stand anyway.

On a whim, I showed Mehran and Saied Shady Beach, and they could talk of nothing else as they saw the potential and wanted in on the deal. They especially wanted the experience of being involved in a development. The downsides were obvious: they were half my age, came from the other side of the world, from a different culture, and I really didn't know them well. Besides, I wasn't a fan of partnerships, so I didn't relish the idea. Yet, they had money. All they had to do was pick up the red telephone and call Dad in Iran.

Jack and I discussed it. Shady Beach would take a staggering amount of money to purchase and develop. The Iranians' money would take some of the strain off of us and we'd retain controlling interest. After much ado, we gave them the nod.

When my brother-in-law, Griff, heard about it, he said we should change the name to Camelot. It took me a few minutes to get the joke. The attorney and his woodpile were left to hang out and dry.

At the closing, Larry Parberry, the seller, came to my office loaded with skepticism and withdrawal symptoms. Of course, I never met a seller who was eager to give up a spot on Payette Lake. Larry was with Morrison-Knudsen and that took him to the Middle East. He claimed the only thing young, male Iranians knew how to do was comb their hair. He was convinced we couldn't succeed and he'd no doubt get the property back. His prediction didn't daunt me. The Iranians showed up and the four of us sat around the conference table.

Before we got down to the business of closing, the Iranians decided they should negotiate the price. My heart went into my throat. I quickly ushered them to the kitchen and told them, "Boys, you can't negotiate after the contract is signed. If you try, you could squelch the deal. So stop it." I discovered later that is what many mid-easterners do. Okay, that is just fine in Iran, but not in America.

I yo-yoed from Boise to McCall and then back to Boise. But that was the only way I could do it. I'd never spend more than a couple of days in McCall before I scooted home. Sometimes, I got a little overwhelmed and felt like I was on a sinking raft in a raging river holding on by my fingernails. Then, I took up Transcendental Meditation and that made all the difference. I'd retreat to a quiet corner in the basement to put in my twenty minutes.

After I took a moment to become comfortable in my chair, I'd close my eyes, put my feet flat on the floor and rest my hands on my lap, palms up. Then I would repeat my mantra under my breath, over and over, not allowing my mind to wander. And if it did, I'd pull it back and continue concentrating on my mantra. And that's how I learned to quit thinking: the secret for relieving tension. Jack was impressed with my success and became a devotee of Transcendental Meditation, too.

When we got home, Jack disappeared in his "drawing" room. He drew up the plat, and the utility and drainage systems. The latter was necessary because the land was riddled with springs. In the process, we discovered that Clem Parberry only had a "summer easement" to access the property. Dr. Nokes owned the property between Shady Beach and Lick Creek Road and had granted that limited easement. I called him from my office and told him I needed a year-round easement, would that be possible? He told me he could meet me at Shady Beach the following Saturday to talk about it.

When we got together, I tried to pin Dr. Nokes down about a year-round easement. He just smiled. He wanted to know what I was getting for the old cabins that had to be removed. Finally, I caught on. "How about two cabins?" I asked. Two cabins in exchange for a year-round easement suited Dr. Nokes just fine. One more hurdle jumped!

Our first challenge was to remove the rest of the summer cabins from the land. At $1,000 each, they were carted off to new lives along the Sesesh River and other destinations around McCall. Todd Schaefer, one of our agents, moved one to a new subdivision and remodeled it. Jack and John dragged one on a low-boy trailer to Pilgrim Cove where it was tucked behind our existing cabin, creating a bedroom, second bath, and a spa room complete with a little wood stove and a six-foot antique footed tub taken out of our downtown office building. This required removing a tree. I was on the phone talking to an agent when Jack interrupted me saying, "I'm sorry." He disappeared and I went right on talking until I realized I wasn't getting any response from the agent and it dawned on me what Jack was trying to tell me. The telephone line was dead. Lumberjacking wasn't exactly Jack's forte.

In the process, John built a turret just big enough to sleep in, over the bedroom. The access was a hinged ladder that came down in the middle of the room. To raise the ladder out of the way, John counter-balanced it with a big tear-shaped rock on the end of a rope that went up and down on an outside cabin wall as the ladder was raised and lowered inside. People walking by often did a double-take.

The lot we intended to keep was decimated by the huge tractors and trucks but it was essential for the contractor to get to the lake and that is what it took. At that juncture, the contractor told me that the sewer district would give Shady Beach the deck that covered the pump, and it would be up to the homeowners to maintain it.

Years later, the deck became unstable and consequently a hazard. I discussed the problem at the homeowners' meeting. Some of the people thought that the sewer district should replace it, but I told them that wasn't going to happen.

"The contractor made it clear at the onset that it would be up to the homeowners to maintain it. I would be happy to talk to the sewer board about how we should go about it," I said. A fellow from California offered to go with me. When I presented our problem to the board, they listened. They said they would send someone out to talk to us. Then the California guy stood up and in a boisterous, snarled voice, he said, "We'll sue the socks off of you if anyone gets hurt on that broken down deck! And that's not just a threat." I wanted to disappear in the woodwork. The board was taken aback. The chairman reiterated what I had already told the homeowners: the upkeep was up to us. Then he adjourned the meeting.

It is funny about the Californians. Most of them were happy to be in Idaho but there were a few who continuously stirred the pot of discontentment. Maybe that came about because Southern California is so congested, they felt they had to fight to get their share. Here, we are more relaxed and adhere to the philosophy of "live and let live." That's one of the things I love about Idaho.

Back in Boise, I had scheduled a series of real estate classes for the agents. I gave lectures on business practices and ethics. I used a set of Tom Hopkins's videos as they contained some good information on the art of selling. But Tom Hopkins reminded me of a carnival barker and he dressed like one right down to the "rug" he wore to hide his baldness. He was someone's idea of what a Realtor should look like, but not mine. I got a kick out of one thing he said: "No matter whether the market is good or bad, if someone asks you how real estate is doing, just say, *unbelievable.*"

I was delighted when Steve Brown came out with a classier rendition of real estate training. I liked his style, manner and approach as it was more refined, yet his methods weren't exactly my style either. I had a little problem when he appeared on one of his videos in a bright red suit, his idea of "dressing for success."

I still had the Payette Lake Sewer District to deal with so I made a quick trip to McCall. In the process of building their homes in Shady Beach were town-folk Bill and Willa Kirk, who were in the insurance business in McCall; and Dr. Brad Gauss, a local dentist, and his wife Marsha, an artist. It was up to me to provide a sewage system by the time their cabins were complete. I had a pretty strong feeling they wouldn't accept an outhouse. I was thankful that it took two years to build anything substantial in McCall because of the short summers and long harsh winters. My race with time was on.

The sewer line was designed to sit below the shoreline around the lake. The problem was, I realized after attending a sewer meeting, that the Chairman of the Sewer Board was against the sewer. Unbelievable! How could the Chairman of the Sewer Board be against the sewer? Well, he was against growth around the lake. If he succeeded in stopping the sewer, we would have to give up a back building lot and pump the effluent up to it and create a septic system. It would be expensive and far from desirable. And, what about the health of the lake? There was no guarantee that a septic system would keep the contaminants from making it down to the water.

Some State of Idaho commissioners decided they had to step in and rectify the situation by going after the Payette Lake Sewer District in court. So it became the State of Idaho and Adelaide McLeod versus the Payette Lake Sewer District.

I enlisted a savvy attorney from Lou Cosho's office. Though the years, I told anyone who would listen, that if I was in deep trouble, Dick Greener was the man.

The Sewer District hired a limnologist from the University of Idaho to tell the court that the lake's water quality would be destroyed by placing the sewer line in the lake. He said it would take ten years or more for the water to clear and the disturbed dirt to settle.

Dick Greener presented an outstanding argument and the court ruled in our favor. This, of course, resulted in the Sewer District's defeat in its attempt to stop the sewer. I could breathe again. Much to my delight, in the spring, after the sewer was installed, the water was crystal clear.

Back in Boise, after I settled a squabble over a commission split, I broke the speed limit as I was late getting to Hillcrest Country Club for a Leeds meeting. I was the founding member and consequently I became the group leader.

My sister, Jane, belonged to a Leeds Club in La Habra, California, and she sang its praises so I felt like it was a worthwhile thing for me to do. Our group consisted of twenty women who owned businesses. Each member was the only one doing her particular type of business so there was no competition between them. Charter members were: Mary Lu Burns, co-owner of Burns' Photographic Studio; Mary Tate who owned Tates' Rents; Mary Search owned a California Closets franchise, another owned the Swim and Run store, one owned a physical therapy facility, another, a dress shop, and so on. When one of us had a problem, she could run it past the rest of us for a possible solution. We discussed how to promote our companies' images, how to increase the size of our businesses, how to hire and fire an employee and many other topics.

Participation in the meetings never waned. We were able to boost each other's morale, help with new ideas, share successes and have that kind of camaraderie that seemed to fit a niche that nothing else could. How nice it was to deal with women, where you were assured mutual respect, unlike the male dominated nature of most businesses.

About this time, I hired a receptionist: a young girl who had a live-in boyfriend. One morning she came into the office literally battered. I couldn't put her at the front desk looking like that.

I wasn't sure just what to do.

Before long, some of the McLeodies (as the agents liked to call themselves) offered to take her place until she healed. They made up a schedule and took turns. It worked because all of them had had a lot of practice filtering phone calls. So they were in their element and we made do.

But that's not all they did. They passed the hat and we gave her money so she could move away from her boyfriend, and then they helped her move. There was no end to the help they were willing to give her. It warmed my heart.

Before much time passed, she went to work for another company. The broker hired her because The Statesman runner, who came to pick up our ads, got the idea she was the advertising arm of our business. Typing the ads was a small part of the picture. She hadn't composed ads, done the art work, the layout or analyzed which properties needed to be advertised. Nonetheless, The Statesman runner gave another real estate company our receptionist's name, which was a tacky thing for the runner to do, and the broker enticed her to move with the promise of a higher salary. I liked the girl and couldn't fault her for wanting to make more money, but they didn't get an advertising specialist: they got a typist. Divine retribution, I thought.

Back in McCall, I made an appointment to talk to a Boise Cascade forester. We had a heavy growth of trees to consider. With his help, I learned about diversifying the variety of trees. If one of the species became diseased, there were healthy trees of another variety to take over.

The forester encouraged me let him harvest some of the biggest trees. I rebelled. We compromised over that issue and I saved a few large ponderosa, fir, and tamaracks that would enhance the building sites for our future buyers.

Then there was the thinning process. If the trees were too close together they become distorted and spindly. When we were through, that property known as Shady Beach wasn't that shady anymore. And one last lesson from the forester: In the mountains, in woodsy areas, a channel of clearing where the sun rays can touch the earth is especially nice on cold days.

We ran our city water line from Five Corners, more than a mile from Shady Beach, and near Pilgrim Cove's entrance. Our cabin was in Pilgrim Cove and I was aware that the State of Idaho Land Department turned the water off in early October so there was no way cabin owners could be there in the winter unless they hauled in water which wasn't likely. Feeling very generous, I offered city water at my cost to the president of the Pilgrim Cove Home Owners' Association.

He turned me down and said something like: "How can I trust Iranians."

"Well, let me tell you, they are trustworthy, and honest," I told him.

"Then they must be Christians."

I bit my tongue. There was nothing else I wanted to say. To this day, more than thirty years later, Pilgrim Cove still doesn't have city water.

Mehran and Saied bought a big road tractor in an effort to do their part and get involved. You can't learn how to operate such a rig overnight and their amateur efforts resulted in our hiring local talent to do the road work -- the land contouring and grading and burying the utilities. We were the first subdivision around the lake to have underground power.

I asked the sewer contractor to put our line in first and he was agreeable. He could see no reason not to. There would be several pumping stations around the lake and Shady Beach would have the first one. After digging a very deep hole and shoring it up with concrete to house the pump at water's edge, they buried the pipeline that would carry the effluent up to Lick Creek Road. The contractor rebuilt the road into Shady Beach and it was in better shape that it had been before.

In 1990, Jack and I built our dream, "Frog Crossing," on the Shady Beach lot we had kept for our own cabin. It was the one and only time we indulged ourselves by doing exactly what we wanted to, despite the cost. We held out for a massive number of wood-framed windows, pickled knotty pine walls and ceiling, huge structural beams, cedar shingle roofing, maple floors and imported Italian and Mexican ceramic tile in the bathrooms and kitchen. A sunroom across the southern end of the structure created passive solar heat that radiated off its slate floor. The cabin was two-stories plus a crow's nest, more than 2,800 square feet, and it slept fifteen, if everyone was friendly. Jack out-did himself: he designed a masterpiece. Light and airy – cozy and inviting, it became our major venue for entertaining and family gatherings for more than twenty-two years.

We designed an area as a small park in the center of the development. It was heavily wooded with small trees and I made a remark in front of the Iranians that the trees would have to go.

Mehran and Saied had recently discovered chainsaws and cut the trees down, leaving stumps about three feet tall. It was an odd sight. When I discovered it, I caught my breath. It looked like we were attacked by drunken beavers. The word got out and townsfolk by the carloads descended on the site to see for themselves if it was really true.

Jack and I became fond of the Iranians and it was so unfair that some people looked at them as the enemy, especially when they were very much against Khomeini.

Unfortunately, it wasn't long before the red telephone line was cut and the Shah was defeated by Khomeini. There would be no more money from Iran. I adjusted Mehran's percentage of ownership, raided the cookie jar and came up with funds to make the books balance. Those were difficult times for Mehran who was greatly concerned for his family. He went to Iran to help them escape.

Seven of his relatives fled from Iran through the Belgian underground, leaving all their possessions behind except for some jewelry sewn in the lining of their clothes. They spent their first summer in the rustic Parberry lodge. What a cultural shock that must have been for them; but how nice it was that they could enjoy the beauty of Payette Lake. They didn't speak English which sadly, limited my ability to know them better.

They fed their garbage to a skunk that lived under the lodge. He got so fat he could barely walk.

His body was more than two feet wide. I caught one of the locals tip-toeing around trying to take a picture of it.

Finally, the cabins were gone and the land was clear except for the lodge and one cabin on the lake that Clem Parberry had sold years before to a man I'd better not name. It was a 50-foot lakefront and an exception to our deed.

I offered to sell this man access to the water line. He refused only to sneak out under the cover of night and highjack water by putting in his own connection. As much as that frustrated me – I was too busy to mess with him.

On the common ground that provided access to the lake, Jack and John built a flagstone walkway followed by a cedar stairway. A system of pipes under the stairs was essential as the runoff was directed to that spot where it was filtered and ran into the lake.

The buyers flocked in. There was no need to advertise. On the strength of our success, the owner of a condominium project – not on the lake – was impressed with our sales and built a multitude of units that became a glut on the market. It took years to absorb them. I guess he hadn't considered that we were lakefront and he was not.

Many people felt that if they chose McCall for their second home, they wouldn't settle for anything short of lakefront. As time went by, it became difficult to find a lakefront property, and if you did find one, it was so spendy few people could afford it.

A builder in Boise, Dave Pavlis, Jean Smith's client, wanted to buy a lot in Shady Beach. It was late December and the snow was deep. We drove to McCall and the three of us cross-country skied into the development which was not easy terrain. Dave, after studying the plat, decided on his lot regardless of the snow and we side-stepped on our skis a mile uphill to Lick Creek Road where Dave's four-wheel drive was parked. The next day, Jean limped into the office and twisted her body in agony as she confessed that she had never been on cross-country skis before. Now, I call that gutsy. A broker revels in that kind of commitment.

One of my agents, T. J Hill, had two sons who were training for the Olympics in cross-country skiing and McCall was where the action was. It worked out nicely as Tom, who was running the McCall office, was anxious to come back to Boise so T.J. took Tom's place.

One day a man and woman came in the office to look for lakefront. T.J. wanted to make a good impression so she took them around the lake by speedboat. T. J. found a wonderful property and they signed an earnest money agreement and gave T.J. a check. They would be in touch with her soon.

Time went by and T.J. became concerned about her sale and she dug out her copy of the check and called the telephone number printed on it. A man answered but T.J. was pretty sure it wasn't her buyer.

"I'm calling about the sale on a Payette lakefront in McCall, Idaho," T. J. said.

Then the voice on the other end said, "I don't know what you are talking about."

T.J. went on to explain in detail. "Damn, they've done it again!" he grumbled. Evidently, he had a daughter who was "not quite right" and lived in an institution in Salem. From time to time, she and her boyfriend managed to escape and go on an escapade. This, obviously, was one of their fantasy trips.

The Vycitals, good friends of ours, decided to sell their cabin on Payette Lake and build on Lake Cascade. They asked me to market it. Lakefronts were scarce and I had a lot of showings. One day, I took my customers by boat to the Vycital cabin as I told them how pure and pristine the lake was. "That is where our drinking water comes from," I said. When we arrived at the dock, there was a gaggle of geese sunning on the dock which was literally covered with goose poop. As I was trying to explain that it would be cleaned up, one of the buyers piped up with, "Yeah, they'll sweep it into the water." Well, wouldn't you know, they decided not to buy a cabin on the lake.

Those geese gave "poop deck" a new meaning.

Shady Beach was an fascinating experience and a profitable one, as well. I enjoyed the Iranians and the caring McCall people. Most of all, I loved the challenge. The Shady Beach residents still marvel about this treasure of a place that is darn near perfect. No other subdivision around the lake has city water and underground power, and the best view on the lake. And to think that Jack and I were instrumental in making that happen.

Not all my real-estate efforts have had such happy endings. Garden Valley was an enlightening experience and a hard blow to my psyche. It's on my list of "Never Do That Again." I graduated from the school of Hard Knocks, cum laude. Yet, that was where I learned to trust my inner voice.

It knew from the onset things were bogus, but I wasn't listening.

I had been talked into investing in a hollow corporation. I soon discovered that the funds were going directly into the instigator's pocket. It's a given that we all have to have our setbacks. It was fortunate that this was just a small disaster. Yet it was for a purpose. It caused me to grow out of my naivety and quit believing that everyone in the world was honest.

The Shape of Things to Come

It was interesting to watch the changes in architecture as my years in real estate rolled by. Architecture seems to mirror what is happening in the world. For instance, the period right after World War II had little architectural merit. With veterans coming home at the end of the war, there was a urgent need for housing. The best of what was built was called Ranch Style: an oblong box, often featuring three bedrooms and a bath and a half. The front door was most always in the middle of the front wall, with the garage on one side and a picture window on the other. The kitchen was predictably behind the living room and there was usually a small eating space in the kitchen. Needless to say, they weren't particularly inspired but builders loved them because of their sameness. They built them and built them, ad nauseam.

It has only been in the last twenty-five years or so that many Boise architects designed houses. Prior to that time they concentrated on churches, schools and commercial structures. There were exceptions, but only a very few. Residential plans were usually rendered by a draftsman.

When the architects began to concentrate on residential design, most of the builders of any merit employed an architect. One of our Boise builders jumped aboard when architects first began designing houses. He was a penurious man and very conservative. After he had the plans in hand, he would remove many of the nuances that the architect had designed and only build what he thought was necessary. His houses were slow to sell: they were predictably mediocre. He just couldn't bring himself to follow the architect's design because that would cost more money. This went on for a few years, and he finally went on a much-needed vacation and left his foreman in charge of the house that was under construction. The foreman followed the architect's plans precisely. This resulted in a roaring success. When the builder came home, he took all the credit although he had very

93

little to do with building the house. It gave him such prestige and notoriety that he was soon considered one of Boise's best builders.

In the fifties, there was a mid-century modern style of more merit. It had a low-gabled roof with considerable overhang. The living room was graced with walls of windows, fireplaces sat in walls of stone, and there was often a flagstone floor somewhere. They were livable and had certain charm. However, the construction was expensive, so a limited number of them were built in Boise.

In the eighties, value was calculated by the size of the house. Buyers often used the square footage to confirm the price with little or no attention to quality. That is likely why housing became so awkwardly big. Any effort to emulate classic architecture fell short.

The stucco Southwestern house made its debut in Boise in the late eighties. It was Boise builders' first worthy attempt to use stucco since the twenties. Somewhat Spanish in style, it featured arches and floor tile, vaulted ceilings and rounded corners with minimum woodwork.

Next came the advent of oversized bathrooms, some as big as a bowling alley. They had a jetted tub, an enormous shower, a walled-off toilet, walls of mirror, double sinks, and were usually adjacent to a huge walk-in closet. There was enough room in them to entertain a dozen friends, leaving room for the dance band. I never could understand why.

The trend to build big kitchens made more sense as it seems to be where people gather when you have company. Yet, when a kitchen gets really big it is a killer to work in when preparing a meal. The range is twenty steps from the sink and the refrigerator is in the next county. The appliances must be stainless steel and imported with such names as Bosch and Viking, the counter-tops: granite and the floor: exotic hardwood. The kitchen has become the fashionable place to entertain. Guests stand swigging their wine, as close to the snacks as is discrete, while their feet go numb. They could be relaxing in the "overstuffed" furniture in the living or family rooms, but that doesn't happen.

I am very happy to say that high-quality residential architecture finally made a resurgence after a long period of dormancy. Housing has become exciting and beautiful. Houses are still big, too big, with overdone baths and large, elaborate kitchens, but real style is surfacing and quality is back. And smaller, more efficient homes are gaining favor nationwide.

As a family project, we developed the land and built thirty-two Craftsman patio homes in Lake Harbor off of State Street called Tivoli Garden. Abandoning the philosophy of "big" in favor of the "not so big house," we used only top-notch materials. We all made our contribution. Jack did the plat, lot design, infrastructure, footprint, and the floor plans.

Intrigued by the Arts and Crafts movement, Tom opted for the bungalow. After a thorough study of Gustav Stickley, the chief proselytizer for the American Craftsman movement, and Craftsman architects early in the twentieth century: Charles Green, Henry Green and Charles Sumner, Tom explained that every little detail, top to bottom, inside and out, had to be true Craftsman. This artisan approach would cost more and take longer to build but we felt it was worth it. Some of the Craftsman style's intricacies had been forgotten and we reintroduced them. There was no competition for our homes on the Boise market or in the West as far as we could discover.

We flew down to Pasadena as we heard there was a street of Arts and Craft houses, only to learn that they had been built in the 1920s and they were all occupied, so it was impossible to view the interiors. The City of Pasadena, and the homeowners involved, took pride in the Craftsman houses and put them on parade and open to the public for a few days every year, but we missed it. Yet our trip wasn't wasted as it was a great opportunity to study the Craftsman exteriors. Their dynamic balance created a sense of harmony, an element seldom seen elsewhere.

There are Boise builders who use Craftsman touches, like slanted pillars near the front door, but there is little follow through. Tom, John and Kevin built the homes and the landscaping fell in my lap, along with downzoning from commercial to residential. Continuity and appropriate detail seemed to make all the difference. A buyer told Tom, "I'd like to live in your piece of art."

It was a very special time for all of us and we were proud of our project. We had too much fun. I was so enamored with what we had done that I am living there now.

There haven't been many houses built in Boise since the recession began. Numerous cases of abandoned infrastructures dot the landscape. Lately, there have been a few new houses being built. Some people regard this as a sign of a healing economy. Maybe, but after years of nothing, some builders just couldn't stand to be idle any longer and built in spite of the economy. Every small glimmer of movement can't be interpreted as a healing economy, even though we'd all like to think so. The economy will get better as there is always change, but it may never be as good as we remember it. I'm glad that I was involved in the best of times.

In the nineties, I recognized my attention needed to be on the big picture. I took a deep breath and turned management of the brokerage over to my trusted Associate Broker, Ann Erstad, so I could spend time and effort in pursuing developments that our company could represent.

Ann's grandfather, James Pinney, had been both Mayor of Boise and Governor of Idaho early in the twentieth century. He also established the beautiful Pinney Theater – one more treasure that has been destroyed in downtown Boise.

Ann seemed to follow in her grandfather's footsteps in knowing how to get where she wanted to go. Her civic interests led her to serve on the board of the Historic Preservation Society, the Idaho Botanical Garden, and other worthwhile endeavors. She carried the stiff demeanor of a school teacher but that was all right: she was bright and ran a tight ship. Her tenure at McLeod came to an abrupt end due to unforeseen circumstances. Ann had planned a trip to the Holy Land with her friend, Betty Gibson. It was all set, but just before they were scheduled to leave Betty suddenly died. That event caused Ann to rethink what she was doing with her life and she retired.

It wasn't long before she discovered she had incurable cancer. When she came home from the hospital, I wanted to go see her but I was so devastated over what had happened to her, I needed support. Jean and Kathi were willing to go with me, so I called Ann and told her the three of us were bringing lunch. She met us at the door dragging her oxygen line. She wore a cute ski hat that covered the fact that her hair had fallen out in the course of her treatment. Tesi, her daughter, brought the hat back from Salt Lake where she had gone to the Olympics. Ann greeted us with a big smile. We ate lunch, making small talk and laughing as women are wont to do, and I almost forgot Ann was dying. By the time we left, I realized, we had come to cheer Ann up, but as it turned out, she was the one who had done the cheering. She was a favorite of mine and I miss her to this day. Losing a close friend is like losing a piece of yourself.

In real estate, time is of the essence. But how does one tune into good timing? All I know is that you must stay alert, with antenna in tune and your creative juices flowing. Be constantly aware of what is happening around you and larger trends out there in the world.

Understand how fragile and volatile it all is. On a daily basis we experience changes that are sometimes subtle, other times dramatic. Whichever, we need to be aware or we won't be the ones who make the sale. In the words of that great Nashville philosopher, Kenny Rogers: "You've got to know when to hold 'em, know when to fold 'em, know when to walk away, know when to run." Is real estate like a poker game? Yes, indeed. You win or you lose -- you make the sale or you don't.

Passion is up there right alongside timing in importance. How do you develop passion? I'm not sure you can. It's as elusive as love. If you have a passion for the real-estate business then nothing can stop you. It's a slam-dunk. Have you ever wondered why some people find success while others who seem to try harder, don't? Perhaps it is the drive to accomplish, or the ability to bring special talents to the plate that motivates those winners. For sure, it has to do with drawing on the very best of you. Making money is good but there needs to be a deeper motivation than that. Passion makes us come alive with an insatiable desire -- that can make all the difference.

Enthusiasm is no substitute for passion, but while you are nurturing passion, you might settle for enthusiasm. If you work at being enthusiastic, you are on a happy road and you will not go unnoticed as people are drawn to happy people and that exercise might help you develop passion if such a thing is possible.

Business is always changing: our one-page Earnest Money Agreement grew to fifteen and then fell back to seven. At first, when I went into the real-estate business in 1970, there were no computers, copying machines, faxes, voice mail, or cell phones. Carbon paper was still relevant. We spent hours driving across town to deliver documents, trying to connect with a listing or selling agent, and attempting to decipher that selling agent's handwritten offer. With the advent of all the technical apparatus, we were able to work smarter and faster; but, like most people, my agents hated change and it took a while for each new innovation to be accepted.

I kept telling my crew that the latest technology would make us more productive. However, technology also took some of the personal, hands-on aspect of real estate away, never to be replaced. In a way, those conveniences were harbingers of what was to come.

Autumn 1999: The word on the street was that with the turn of the century, we would no longer be doing business as we had been: there would be a drastic change. How could anyone know that? It made no sense to me.

Yet oddly enough, the soothsayers were right. The new mantra became that onerous word: "big." Small companies were merging with other small companies; large companies gobbled up small companies and in a frenzy, aggressively wooed agents with enticing promises that were seldom kept. The cookie was that with size, the bigger companies had access to technical support systems that were not available to small companies, allowing them to outdo business as they knew it.

Agents moved their licenses to board the millennium train. The day of the small companies was waning. Then came a period of mega mania: a monopoly-minded sort of gluttony. Some people actually believed, if it wasn't unwieldy oversized, it wouldn't work.

Fifteen years ago, in Ada County, Idaho, 70 agents would be considered a large real estate company. Today, Silver Creek Real Estate has 763 agents while Keller-Williams has 561.

It is interesting to note that these two companies are both considered newcomers on the Boise real estate scene. Coldwell-Banker-Tomlinson Group has 256 agents. The smallest and oldest company of the group that is working on mega-growth is Group One with 164 agents.

The way these companies are structured, they have to rely on a huge number of agents to make their companies viable.

I had no desire to be part of it and in 2004 I sold my business. There was no longer time in this fast moving business world for words like ethics, integrity, and accountability, and they fell out of use. I felt like a foreigner lost in a strange place, a place without soul. I wondered if I was the only one who hated it.

It is my theory that some techie in this Brave New World had done the numbers and figured out that every agent had a potential of X dollars. Multiply that by lots of bodies and you, president of the company, would be in the mega bucks. Yet, how does a brokerage of two hundred, three hundred, or even seven hundred agents make this business work? From what I have gathered: <u>painfully</u>. The probability of compromising quality was almost a certainty. When you are part of a large corporation, it seems that "big" has a way of dumbing you down and that can result is a mediocre performance.

At first, the change seemed to work and we saw new highs in market values; but that bubble soon burst and the big change coincided with a staggering fall into the worst downturn since the Great Depression: the Great Recession. Numerous developers and builders were left holding the bag if they were caught in the middle of a project. Business was painfully slow and agents dropped out, while those who hung on were seldom making a living. In time, a phenomenon occurred inside some of those big companies.

Some agents within a big company hired a handful of struggling agents to work for them at the clerical scale. One agent comes to mind, who created such a company and is seldom in the office but is playing golf, skiing or cruising the world. She has a cell phone that creates the illusion that she is in town and is available at the drop of a hat. Her staff keeps the money rolling in. She has succumbed to playing the numbers game.

By the numbers game, I mean a maneuver like throwing the cards in the air to see how may land face up with the caveat that you need to have lots of cards. This scheme might not have worked if the market wasn't so slow. But there were agents wanting to eat and a pittance is better than nothing.

The advent of "big" was not confined to real estate but spread to the corporate world as well, including the federal government which ballooned in size during the last ten years. When people inside a growing company become a number and not a name, accountability seems to lag. Big box companies, such as Walmart, sprung up in our landscape, and franchises flourished as Ma and Pa businesses sadly disappeared. There are jolly few home-owned businesses left in Boise. I patronize them in the hope it will give them a bit more staying power.

There are some encouraging signs that "bigger is better" is on its way out. There was a big school in New York City that had to close its doors because students were out of control. The students were no longer referred to by name, they became a number. The school was so big that the right hand didn't know what the left hand was doing and as it lost it's control, accountability ceased to exist. Because of the mayhem the school became dangerous and the school district couldn't find teachers who were willing to deal with it. Then some visionary had a solution. By dividing the school down the middle and creating two separate campuses, and smaller schools, the students became receptive and the havoc disappeared. The teachers were willing to teach there, once accountability returned. "Big" was clearly the culprit.

In real estate, there are other goals beyond making money. If we are looking for personal satisfaction in what we do; there needs to be integrity, a hands-on approach, and a sense of commitment to our trusting clients whose welfare depends on the quality of our performance.

The question is, can a mega-sized company deliver such services? It seems problematic. How can there be room for that on their greed-driven agenda?

It is my theory "big" is instrumental in the current mess our country is in. Call me old fashioned, but I liked business as it used to be. I agree some of the changes are positive but I get the feeling that the way things are, we are on a fast track to total chaos. I truly believe if the virtues came back into vogue, if we practiced things like humility, kindness, justice and integrity, the world would heal. But you can't do that in an oversized company, whose mission statement is more, more, more.

It's hard to see our country falling apart. Some folks are saying we should give the power back to the states and put a limit on corporations, both in size and in number, as it used to be. Maybe they have something there.

Business needs to be accountable. We need to change our direction. Instead of concentrating on quantity, we could do better to concentrate on quality. Imagine what it would mean to change things from what they are to what they could be. We need to return to traditional virtues if we want to leave the kind of world our children and grandchildren deserve. Aristotle once said, "We are what we repeatedly do. Excellence, then, is not an act but a habit."

The pendulum swings and reaches a point at the top where things go crazy: that is where I think we are now. But one thing we can be sure of, it will swing back and hopefully come to rest in that place of well being. I'm sticking around for that.

One last reflection: I loved those years I spent in real estate. They were more gratifying than you can possibly imagine. My leadership was not a right – it was a privilege. A heartfelt "thank you" to my agents and my clients who contributed to that, and to Jack who stood beside me, put up with me, and was my cheerleader from the beginning to the end.